BALANCE

ME

BALANCE ME

A REALIST'S GUIDE

—— to a ——

SUCCESSFUL LIFE

MATT DeCOURSEY

R_B
Realist Books

$$R_B$$

Realist Books

7235 West 162nd Terrace, Stilwell, KS 66085

ISBN-13: 978-0-692-81180-1
ISBN-10: 0-6928-1180-X
Library of Congress Control Number: 2016960816

CONTENTS

SECTION TWO:
UNDERSTANDING YOUR
PERSONALITY AND OTHERS' (DiSC)

Section Three:
All Things Marriage and Family

Section Four:
Other Important Relationships (Friends, Coworkers, and Yes, Ourselves)

Section Five:
Creating Financial Balance

SECTION SIX:
KEEPING IT PROFESSIONAL

SECTION SEVEN:
BALANCING YOUR MIND AND BODY

INTRODUCTION

IN TODAY'S ever-complicated world, the terms "life balance" and "work-life balance" invoke plenty of curiosity and opinions. Everybody *wants* one but too often it feels daunting, unrealistic, or even impossible to attain. *Balance Me* begs to differ. But first let's get a few things clear:

1. Making real change in your life is not an easy process.

2. Change involves acknowledging that you might be part of the problem.

3. True improvement and lasting change involve time, then periodic review and adjustment.

Starting from these three simple truths, *Balance Me* can create change in your life now and forever. Who can benefit from this book? ANYONE! Whether you are a busy professional, a stay-at-home mom, or someone wishing to achieve their goals without sacrificing well-being, this book is for you!

What you stand to gain is up to you. Every reader has a different set of goals, problems to address, and motivating factors that drive a desire for some kind of change. Not all parts of this book are going to directly relate to your personal story. But many sections will seem like they are written just for you. My goal is that at a bare minimum you will be able to improve your decision-making skills and better understand the WHY of your current situation.

The answer is through making what often times will be small but highly effective changes to your habits, decision-making process, and daily planning. You will learn how to evaluate the value of your actions and then how to replace low-value activities with ones that ultimately move you toward the things that you want in life. By teaching you how to break big tasks, problems, goals, and changes into small pieces, we will build a systematic plan for getting you where you want or need to be.

Let me be more specific. Most people look at their goals and desires as BIG things. And by big I mean one major event or achievement. The reality is your goals and desires and achieving them are in fact a series of small, easily achievable tasks, actions, or changes. We're going to challenge the way you look at problems and instead see solutions. And defining your new path toward balance will occur over whatever duration of time YOU choose. The more you try, the faster change can occur. *Balance Me* provides you with all the necessary tools to make it possible.

Are you with me and ready for growth and change? Let's go!

SECTION ONE:

SET YOURSELF UP FOR SUCCESS

MATT DECOURSEY

WELCOME TO *Balance Me*, a series of thought-provoking exercises, information, and reality checks that will have a positive effect on the personal, professional, and physical elements of your life. My goal is to help you consider and evaluate the daily decisions you make and show how choices can affect the chance at happiness and success within your own definition. Some exercises will stand out and apply to you more than others. But each offers a useful perspective. I can't make you use everything provided here, but it's yours for the taking. And it may surprise you.

Balance Me was created for real people with real lives and responsibilities. It understands that we are human and that sometimes reality, not self-improvement programs, dictates what occurs in your life. There is no silver bullet solution for improving your life balance. The answer is almost always a collection of small changes that lead to big improvements. Look at it like a jar of spare change. It doesn't seem like much when you add a few nickels and dimes here, a quarter there, but you're genuinely surprised when later you take a full jar to the change counter and discover the total number of dollars accrued! *Balance Me* is designed to help you get control over your situation, one handful of change at a time. There isn't a start and completion date but more of a start date and then an ongoing ability to better assess parts of your life.

As you work through the insightful exercises ahead, it's important to remember that these are *not* tests. There are no right or wrong answers—simply answers that apply to you. What you get out of *Balance Me* may be different than what the next reader gets. It's a personalized journey. Whether you go through the program in detail or simply skim through what grabs you, I am 100 percent positive that the new method of evaluation will change the way you think about your personal, professional, and physical life and have a profound impact on your decision-making process.

Creating efficiencies and understanding the value of your current actions compared to other options is the key to getting what you want. *And it is a lot easier than you might think!* With slight variations the process is similar for each category. But in the end, you will have to address each category in order to create a balanced life.

The Three P's of Life Balance: Personal, Professional, and Physical

Your life consists of three general categories: Personal, Professional, and Physical.

The **Personal** category involves activities with your family and friends or solo—things like hobbies, watching television, going to a baseball game, or going to church. In short, it's most of the things you do away from work.

The **Professional** category includes everything centered around your job or a business you own—whatever it is that you do to provide for yourself and your family. This includes time at work, commuting, attending after-hours networking opportunities, any business travel, and even business-related errands like picking up dry cleaning.

The **Physical** category is all the things that relate to your mental and physical well-being. This includes exercising, preparing proper diets, what you do to mitigate stress—whatever activities you do to stay healthy. It also includes the amount of time and effort it takes to deal with physical problems that have already manifested in your life for whatever reason.

Any effort you expend will be directed toward one of these three categories. When we assess where your efforts are being used, we'll use the term "effort points." This is an easy way to quickly and effectively assess where your current balance (or *imbalance*) in life exists.

Now that we've defined the three primary categories, it's important to understand their intertwined relationship. People often ask me, "What is the perfect level of balance?" There is no right answer to this question. Balance and happiness will be different for everyone. It really comes down to finding the mix that works *for you*.

Regardless of where life balance exists for individuals, it is essential to recognize that a large imbalance among these three categories will eventually lead to big problems. For example, let's say you're spending 80 percent of your time and energy on your profession, which leaves maybe 15 percent of your effort to your personal life and 5 percent to your physical life.

While you might be able to maintain this in the beginning, eventually your personal, professional, and physical life will seek to balance each other. Our bodies and souls naturally crave balance. Areas that aren't receiving proper attention will attempt to force some level of balance. And if resisted—or impossible—the result can be damaging to another or even *all* categories.

So if 80 percent of effort is spent on work, your personal and physical will begin to suffer: there's little time leftover for family, friends, and your health. The longer this imbalance exists, the more severe the correction can be.

How do the categories begin to balance themselves out? In the scenario I just described, a likely outcome to spending so much of your time working and so little of it maintaining your physical wellness would be your getting some kind of negative health issue such as high blood pressure, or even a heart attack. In the event that this occurs you will be *forced* to expend more effort addressing the negative physical results produced by this neglected imbalance in your life.

Let me give you a different example: say 70 percent of your effort is being placed on your personal life. You have a tendency to spend a lot of time going out for drinks with your friends, staying up late at night focusing on social activities. Consequently, your time at work may suffer. This leads to a lower level of income from missed work. As a result, the effects are likely to take a toll on your personal life. You may find yourself without a job at the expense of your personal life. It's kind of hard to argue that this will not have an impact on your professional life while also creating high levels of stress in your physical life.

Let's do our first evaluation exercise and get an estimate of where *you* currently put your efforts. During this exercise you will make a general estimate of where your efforts are being allocated. Take a realistic look at the personal, professional, and physical elements of your life as they are now and assign effort points (one point per 1 percent of your estimated effort) to each of the three categories for a combined total of 100. There is no scoring 80 out of 100; nor is there 110 out of 100.

WHERE MY CURRENT EFFORTS GO:

PERSONAL   _____

PROFESSIONAL   _____

PHYSICAL   _____

= 100

Now look at your self-scoring. Are you surprised? Does your life feel out of balance? Do you have a desire to change that?

If the answer was yes to any of the questions I just asked, then what *is* your desired life balance? Answering this next question will give you a lot of insight into what your real goals and priorities are.

WHERE I'D LIKE MY EFFORTS TO GO:

PERSONAL   ____

PROFESSIONAL   ____

PHYSICAL   ____

= 100

This exercise gives you a basic idea of where you are and where you'd like to be. It doesn't have to be an exact measurement and it can change from day to day, week to week. What's important is that you start to get a basic understanding that imbalance exists. You have officially taken a first step toward making significant change in your life. Congratulations! Now let's learn a bit more about ourselves and build on this.

TRUTH: Balance Is Always a Work in Progress

During the process of creating *Balance Me*, I talked to many people about the importance of finding balance in our personal, professional, and physical life. The most popular question I was asked was, "Is *your* life in balance?" Most of the time I grinned and shook my head no. Achieving a continued balance in your life is rare. When you *do* find yourself in a state of near or perfect balance, enjoy it, hang onto it, and mentally catalog exactly what you did to get there. The reality is that it's unlikely to last a prolonged amount of time. But that's okay. It's just the way balance works. I like to envision a child's toy top. When spun, it starts out upright and balanced with a tight rotation, then begins to wobble, only to fall on its side. At this point you can leave it on its side, or choose to give it another spin.

ARE *YOU* THE PROBLEM?

It's time to step back and take a good hard look at yourself. Self-improvement is hard, but you're going to have an impossible time moving forward if you can't see or refuse to take responsibility for your problems. Of course it's a lot easier to blame others for the failures and constant upheaval around your life. But by accepting that you're a part of the problem and accepting responsibility for your actions, you can start working on the solution. You have control over the way you behave, so when you make an effort to shape up and get what you really want out of life, you'll begin to see the rewards. Remember: if you're the problem, you're also the solution.

Change is not easy. It requires courage, honesty, and foresight. Sitting there and hoping things will change is not enough. I have had multiple conversations with friends and business owners over the years who waited far too long to address tough subjects. Perhaps you've heard this phrase: *the only constant in life is change.* It's true and it's inevitable. Seasons change, relationships change, our thoughts and opinions change. Sometimes we choose it and other times it's forced upon us. Typically, people try to avoid change because they fear the unknown. What's interesting about this is that often the unknown is a path that we know good and well we should go down, but we're so stuck in a comfortable way of failing that we sit back and do nothing about it.

A common example: you've smoked for years. You know exactly where that path leads and you've said numerous times that you're going to quit smoking. It's not going to be easy. Your biggest fear isn't when you no longer crave a cigarette—it's fear of the effort along the way, not knowing what that experience will be like. Some obstacles inside you put up roadblocks in the form of excuses. You have to be willing to take action and move out of your comfort zone. With the right commitment and dedication, by letting go of your fears and making changes, you'll find that you're a lot happier.

I said it earlier and it bears repeating here: get a mindset that *small changes can equal big results.* You don't have to make enormous change all at once. Once you see the positive impact of smaller changes, I bet you won't hesitate to make more!

GETTING YOURSELF OUT OF THE WAY

So what's stopping you from getting what you want? It's probably the inability to get yourself out of the way. What does that mean? Getting yourself out of the way means understanding that you can be your own worst enemy. If asked if you are your own worst critic, would you most likely say "Yes"? I bet you would. This can come in a variety of forms. Perhaps it's the manifestation of negative thoughts. Or the self-limiting belief that you are unable to accomplish the things you desire or that certain outcomes in your life are impossible. This is probably one of the most difficult parts of our thought process to fix and maintain on a regular basis.

So how do we adjust this? The first thing to do is to consciously catch yourself limiting your outcomes with negative or unproductive thought patterns. If you find yourself saying in your own head, *I'm not smart enough to do that*, or maybe *I'll never have a lot of money*, then you are absolutely getting in your own way when it comes to improving your situation. When you find yourself having limiting or negative thoughts, the best way to enable change is to use the powerful concept of **replacement**. This entails substituting certain negative thoughts, actions/reactions, situations, and other self-limiting behaviors with ones that produce positive results. With this game-changing technique you'll be on your way to making small changes that can equate to remarkable improvements across your life.

For example, instead of saying, "Man I feel terrible," say, "I feel great!" At that moment you might not feel the best you've ever felt. The irritable feeling won't magically go away in an instant. But by reminding yourself and reinforcing a different—and more positive—thought process, you can begin to create a positive outcome when it comes to your general sense of well-being. Eventually it will help train your mind to understand that you *can* achieve the results you desire.

Here's a more detailed example of that scenario. Amy has friends who run marathons and she thinks she'd be interested in running one too someday. But she says to herself, *I'm overweight; there's no way I can run a marathon.* By continually telling herself this, she is subconsciously removing the desire to even jog in short tolerable intervals. If Amy instead said to herself, *I can run a marathon,* then regardless of her ability to actually do so she might, at the most minimal level, be able to begin training by distance walking, then gain enough confidence to try jogging a few blocks. By replacing the ultimate goal with increasingly attainable steps, she's enabling a path toward the larger task of in-depth training necessary to complete the twenty-six-mile race.

Another example I run into quite a bit when I speak to individuals is the desire to open and manage a small business. I hear statements such as, "I don't think I could ever do that!" Or "It's just not the right time for me to start a business." Again, these are all self-limiting beliefs. The fact is anyone can achieve this goal in a very short period of time. And the magical "right time" is never going to come. You can create unlimited excuses as to why now isn't the right time to do what you really want to do in life. Whether you have been planning and saving for this moment for years or two weeks, it is going to require steps into the unknown. I am not saying that you shouldn't be prepared. In fact, please *do* be prepared. Just understand that with every choice you have action or an excuse. You can remember this as A(ction)—C(hoice)—E(xcuse), or simply A-C-E.

THE IMPORTANCE OF SETTING GOALS

It's hard to hit a target that you can't see. If you don't clearly define what it is that you want, then is it realistic to expect it to happen? Here is where the small, simple action of setting goals can have a dramatic effect on your decisions and actions.

What is a goal? By definition it's something positive you envision, then plan and commit to achieve. Some have deadlines, like going to a certain destination before you are forty, or they may be ongoing, such as reaching various financial milestones throughout your working life. Goals can be long-term, like the financial example, or short-term like the trip. They can even be daily.

Writing down your goals is the first step toward successfully reaching them. Goals only kept in your mind are far more likely to be buried within the other twenty-five hundred thoughts per hour that the average human experiences. Writing them down forces us to pay attention and avoid being vague.

A study on human behavior took place at Harvard University between 1979 and 1989.[1] In it graduates of the MBA program were asked, "Have you set clear written goals for your future and made plans to accomplish them?" The results:

1. Only 3 percent had written goals and plans.
2. 13 percent had goals but not in writing.
3. 84 percent had no specific goals at all.

Ten years later Harvard interviewed members of the prior study again and the results:

1. The 13 percent who had goals but not in writing were earning on average twice as much as the 84 percent who had no specific goals at all.
2. The 3 percent who had written goals and plans were earning on average *ten* times as much as the other 97 percent of graduates. The only difference between the groups is the written clarity of the goals they had for themselves.

Recording one's goals appears well worth the minimal effort!

---

[1] Mark H. McCormack, *What They Don't Teach You at Harvard Business School* (New York: Bantam, 1986).

Earlier you quantified the current personal, professional, and physical elements of your life. After reviewing the result, you then reassessed those three elements and assigned the percentage of time and energy where you *want* your efforts to go. That action was an example of setting a goal. What we're going to do now is clarify specific goals that will help you achieve more positive balance in your life. To begin, divide a sheet of paper into three columns (personal, professional, and physical) and then list a long-term and short-term goal for each category.

Hints:

What is something that you would like to spend more time doing?

What is something that you would like to spend less time doing?

Now list at least five things that need to occur in order for each goal to happen, no matter how big or small. Feel free to list more if you wish.

Now answer the following questions:

Why are you not currently achieving these goals?

What are some of the things that cause you stress, anxiety, or worry?

(This can be as simple as listing things, people, or situations.)

What are a few actions or changes that could help alleviate each concern?

What do you think might be the best way to take action when it comes to improving each scenario?

Okay, now that you have a few positive changes to shoot for let's figure out how to get it started. But before we move on there are a couple truths to establish:

1. Change is tough and takes time and effort.

2. Success demands payment in advance.

TRUTH: Change Is Tough

Establishing goals and creating a plan to achieve them puts you ahead of the majority of people. Rest assured, it is common at this point to feel a bit overwhelmed. This happens because you now realize all the effort and actions needed to get what you want. Instead, consider that you are now officially in motion toward your goal. The more you put into your plan, the more you will get out of it. Change is tough. That isn't going to change and there isn't a way around it. Accepting this fact helps.

Start thinking of yourself as a doer. You are no longer someone who settles for the status quo. Everything you want is right in front of you. It is now up to you to go get it. I have had a lot of people tell me that I am "lucky" because I managed to find success in lots of different categories of my life. The problem is, I don't believe in luck as a trait that some have and others don't have. Many people define luck as "preparation and opportunity crossing paths." I do as well. I want you to consider this as you continue to move toward your goals. Put yourself in a position of being *prepared* for opportunities.

TRUTH: Success Demands Payment in Advance

It's true and there is no real way around this. If you want to find success with whatever it is that you are doing or aim to do, then you will have to put in the time and effort required. The more difficult the task, the higher the price. Success is measured in so many different ways: financial, social, charitable, romantic, physical, familial, or any variety of views we choose to take. By understanding that you can control your destiny through daily improvement and awareness of your current condition then you too can find success through whatever measurement you choose. However, no matter what course you set there will be some kind of upfront payment required when it comes to effort.

Consider professional athletes. Many people will look at them and say that they are gifted, lucky, or fortunate to be where they are. In reality they have spent a lifetime working and practicing to be the best at what they do. Hours, days, weeks, months, even YEARS of practice have gotten them to a level of expertise and success. This is a clear example of success demanding payment in advance.

Examples of success demanding payment in advance are EVERYWHERE you find success. The greatest part about it is that it is something YOU can control. While some cases might require some level of talent or physical stature, most don't. In fact, even in people who might naturally seem to have talent or physical attributes that most don't, you will still find that they have dedicated amazing amounts of time, effort, emotion, and thought to becoming the best at what they do. So how does this relate to you? It means if you are willing to pay the price, then you too can become an expert at being successful.

Because I feel so strongly about this concept, I want to continue to define what payment in advance is often referred to as. Commonly used terms like dedication, drive, ambition, obsession, diligence, self-discipline, and practice all come to mind. So when you commit yourself to achieving greater balance in your life, as well as setting goals and then taking action, you are just practicing being the way you want to be.

The bottom line is if you truly want to find success, avoid shortcuts. Don't sacrifice the long term on the altar of the immediate. Acknowledge and accept these concepts as fact, then get to work. Period.

ACCOUNTABILITY AND RESPONSIBILITY

What is accountability? For me, the term accountability is closely related to responsibility. It not only means being responsible for something but also ultimately being answerable for your actions and decisions. You fully own the situation. It's sometimes hard to hold ourselves accountable for others' decisions that impact us. But at the same time, if your husband or wife or even boss makes a decision and it has an effect on you, whether large or small, there's still a level of accountability that needs to be taken.

There are certain factors you have to accept as your responsibility—your children for one. Your own actions first and foremost are most important. Why? If you don't hold yourself accountable, you start making excuses for why nothing went right for you. You begin to trade in what I call the "economy of falsehoods." Imagine a young lady getting a speeding ticket. She was clearly driving fifty miles an hour in a thirty-five-miles-an-hour zone and—no surprise—she got a ticket. "How dare he give me a ticket!" she complains. "I can't believe he did that to me!" She accepts no accountability or responsibility for her action.

Responsibility and accountability are a big part of growth and maturity in your personal, professional, and physical life. If you're overweight and don't have a true medical reason for it, you have to have some accountability that you probably consumed a lot of calories and didn't exercise. The first step is accepting that your habits need to change. Only then can you start to create a successful plan.

So answer the question: Do you hold yourself accountable for your actions and decisions? If not, you're not being honest with yourself. The ability to hold yourself accountable for the decisions you make is a sign of maturity and is necessary for change. Being dishonest in this regard is a form of self-deception. Constantly blaming others for things that aren't going well in your life shows a lack of accountability on your part.

Often people are afraid to say something as simple as "I really messed that up and I need to do a better job next time." The ability to hold yourself accountable to coworkers, friends, and family in various situations in life is a form of honesty with yourself. It is essential if you want to find ways to improve. It's okay to admit you were wrong. Actually in a lot of situations others will have a greater respect for you when they see you take accountability and responsibility for your actions.

Being accountable and taking responsibility for your actions allows you to own the situation. Not doing so does the opposite, allowing the situation to own you. For every decision you make, are you willing to accept that *you're* the one who made the decision and must live with the consequences? If the outcome doesn't turn out the way you want it to, it's not the fault of someone else.

What's Calling You?

When I ask, "What is calling you?" I am really asking, "What is distracting you?" Let's use the example of someone who can't seem to put their phone down (no pun intended about what's calling you!). Someone who lives their whole life with their face to their phone, whether it's for tweeting, checking Facebook, sending and responding to e-mails, or constantly checking text messages. They're not present in the here and now, clearly putting everything else aside for whatever is going on in that phone. I'm not saying you shouldn't use that media, but you have to start to be responsible and accountable for the fact that whatever is going on with the phone better be pretty important. Sadly, it's probably not. Blabbing, gossiping, flirting, you name it—it's most likely not a high-value activity. Now start totaling up all of these actions you should be holding yourself accountable for; it adds up to a whole lot that can have an adverse effect on your personal, professional, and physical life.

If you're at work and sending forty personal text messages a day, don't be surprised if you don't have that job much longer. Look at the accountability on that. If one of your goals is to have a higher level of achievement on a professional level, put the phone down. Turn social media off.

Jump, Then Build Wings

I like to say, "Sometimes you just have to jump, then build wings!" At some point, no matter what else is going on, if you're going to do something that's a big change in your life, you're going to have to wrap your arms around this theory. Very few things in life guarantee sure results. There's risk in just about everything we do. You have to learn to embrace it. If you fear change and risk, and your goal is to start a business, you may need to go back and reconsider if that is in fact the right thing for you to do. If you don't handle anxiety, stress, and pressure well, I'm going to tell you something you might not want to hear: you might not be the greatest business owner. If it sounds confusing that I stressed the need for planning and consideration and now I'm telling you to jump and figure it out, that's not what I'm saying. I'm talking about a leap of faith. Tell me how a leap of faith is any different than jumping and building wings and I'll listen, but I guarantee when it's reduced down, it's very similar.

So. . . looking for "the right time"? You might be waiting for a while. This is usually the top excuse people use as to why they aren't taking the first step toward a goal. You can almost always come up with a reason WHY it isn't the right time. Yes, there are in fact situations and circumstances that could deter your success, but whether you prepared for ten years or ten days the changes, opportunities, and goals you seek will still require a little "F#$% it, let's go for it" on your part.

THE "RIGHT TIME" MYTH

I want to reinforce the message that as you progress through the *Balance Me* program just going through the strategies one time may give you some tools and cause you to change your thought process and lead you to a more deliberate course of action. But you have to keep practicing! You have to keep allowing the concepts to enter your thought process. You can make short-term change but if you don't keep practicing the things that enable that, you're going to regress right back to where you were.

We keep talking about the importance of goals. But it's just as important to start prioritizing them. If you ask people why they aren't doing what they *really want* to be doing, the response in most cases will be some variation of "it's not the right time." If your goal is to start a business and I ask why aren't you doing it, of one hundred people I survey, eighty of them will tell me it's just not the right time. But guess what? *The right time never comes.* If that's the way you're going to think about it, you're probably never going to start that business. You're always going to find an excuse or a reason why it's not the "right" time.

Of course there are times that aren't the *best* time. You probably don't want to open the doors to a new business two days before your wife is going to have a baby. Maybe you are buried in debt, have health problems, are about to move, or need to focus on straightening out other parts of your life. But overwhelmingly *most* are an excuse used to justify why you're not doing what you want to be doing. Is it the right time to quit your job and jump into this new business you want to start? Maybe not. However, you can still be taking steps toward starting your business that don't require it to meet all the specific and necessary criteria for you to dive right in.

Your Plan Now Includes Success

If you don't have a plan, then you plan to fail. You have probably heard that warning prior to now and it's true. When you set goals, you start creating your plan. Planning helps you organize your thoughts, shape your future actions, and prepare you for the good, the bad, and sometimes the ugly.

When things get a little too complex, people begin to justify why something is or is not working for them. Justification is a really dangerous thing—it's a crutch. One of the biggest things people will say in regard to not getting what they want in life or achieving their goals is they don't have enough time: "I just don't have enough hours in the day." Well guess what? Everyone in the world has the same finite twenty-four hours in their day. Every day. It is up to each of us to choose how we *use* that time.

28

Another great example of justification is the person who struggles with personal finance yet still goes shopping for stuff they don't even need or can't afford because of the self-sabotaging thought, *I work hard; I deserve this!*

Acting before thinking can destroy progress in achieving your short-term or long-term goals. Sometimes it's the "little" impulsive decisions that can, as a result of unintended consequences, cause as much grief as the major ones. Impulsive decisions affect health: watching television instead of going out and getting some exercise, eating a double cheeseburger instead of a salad, drinking too much because your friends are. Impulsive decisions stem from the "now" mentality that is all too common in today's world. This encourages the belief that you can have everything you want NOW without considering that the other side of that equation is LATER. The most common term for this is *self-discipline*. I define self-discipline as doing the things you need to do at the times you LEAST want to do them. Without developing some level of awareness of the need and value of self-discipline you will find yourself continually pushing your goals further away.

Planning forces you to organize your thinking and identify the main issues preventing you from achieving success. And thinking through what you need to do saves you time in the long run—it makes your objectives clear and specific. When you put together a plan, you can sit back and take a good look at it then identify any flaws or weaknesses to make corrections.

Plus if you focus on a few of your objectives rather than trying to accomplish everything at once, you will concentrate on using your resources more wisely.

Planning tip: Don't just plan for the "sunny day," plan for the "rainy day" too. You are more likely to find the "rainy day" plan useful if or when you need it.

Opportunity Cost

In the first pages of this book you were told that you would be presented with various tools and exercises that would help improve your decision-making. So here we are at one of the most powerful concepts I have encountered: *opportunity cost.* As you read through this section please take a few moments throughout and try and perform a couple of simple comparisons and calculations. Learning how to do this on the fly can be one of the greatest changes you make regarding your overall thought process.

Successful people have learned the importance of determining which tasks are high priorities and which ones are not, whether it's in their personal, professional, or physical life. Being able to choose the highest-value tasks in a situation will result in a more effective plan of action and prevents you from wasting time and energy on low-value activities.

The definition of *opportunity cost* is the value of the forgone option in any decision-making process—the value of something that must be given up to acquire or achieve something else. Opportunity cost can't always be measured in equal units.

Opportunity cost can be applied to anything you do and can have multiple answers. In some situations, looking at the multiple choices you *didn't* choose could add together to yield its own opportunity cost. It's an important thing to consider in life and in business because it's a pretty good measurement for what you're missing out on.

Opportunity cost is a pretty basic principle; however, training yourself to quickly assess it before making decisions is something that takes time and practice. The reason that it is tricky is that often times there is no "right" answer.

Take this example in the professional area: A business owner has the chance to go to a networking meeting where the participants are his peers as well as prospective clients. The other option is to reorganize the files in his warehouse so he can free up cluttered space. What is the value—or opportunity cost—of each option?

The networking meeting provides the chance for the owner to gain insight from his peers and new business through meeting potential clients. Therefore value equals business insight, new business, and/or new revenue. The warehouse project provides the feeling of being more organized and possibly having more space and organization in the warehouse.

So which is more valuable?

Most people would say the networking option. The business exists to make sales and revenue; therefore, this option has more possible value than the second choice. The only way the warehouse option would be more valuable to the business is if the cleared space presented or did create the ability to generate revenue.

That was a pretty easy one. Most of the time this measurement isn't as clear-cut. It might involve you or others having to choose from a variety of routes, deciding which is most beneficial.

Opportunity cost can also value whether you work or play. Whether you realize it or not, you have been making opportunity cost-related decisions your entire life. These are decisions that only you can determine are correct or incorrect, or maybe neither. The bottom line is through training yourself to instinctively calculate and assess opportunity cost, you make yourself more aware in each of the three P categories. The opportunity cost of staying late at work is not spending as much time with your family. However, it's possible that your family as a whole might benefit from the extra income you receive from this or perhaps the business your family owns improves as a result. Only you can truly say these decisions are right or wrong.

Another practice example: you're a contractor and must choose between two available jobs that will take the same amount of time. Maybe you like doing one task more than the other but it pays a lot less. Your opportunity cost is the difference between the higher-paying job and the lower-paying one. Sometimes it's dollars versus dollars, but what you'll find a lot of times is that it's experience versus experience.

Opportunity cost is a debate you can have with anything. It can be a very powerful thought process. On the simplest level, it's an avenue for thought before making a choice and a great tool for help determining *which* choice to make.

High Value Versus Low Value

Any type of activity in your life has some kind of relative value compared to the alternatives. You probably agree that an hour of work where you earn a wage is more valuable than an hour spent mindlessly watching reality television. Some kind of value can be assigned to everything you do.

Activities that move you toward achieving your goals, needs, and desires meet the definition of *high value*. These actions also at the same time create a feeling of balance in themselves. Common examples are exercise, quality time with your family, productive time at work, educational activities, improving some part of your financial situation, or even helping others achieve their goals. If you are being honest with yourself then you intuitively know which actions are high value and which aren't. If you find yourself making excuses as to why something is high value then it probably isn't.

Low-value activities might include watching television, overusing social media, and gossiping with friends or coworkers—anything that brings negative results into your life or actions that push you further from your goals.

My aim is to help you learn to identify the value of chosen courses of action and then start making small but effective replacements that, over time, will result in your getting the outcome you want.

Ask yourself, what are some *high-value* activities in your life? Remember these are specific actions or activities that move you toward one of your goals or help you achieve better overall balance.

Examples of High-Value Activities
- Any action that moves you closer to achieving one of your goals
- Any action that creates a better sense of balance among the three P's
- Actions and activities that produce positive gains in more than one of the three P's
- Education or training courses
- Helping friends, family, or coworkers achieve their goals
- Creating an action plan at the beginning of each day
- Staying focused on activities that produce the best possible results
- Exercise
- Proper diet

What are some of the *low-value* activities in your life? These are actions or blocks of time where you don't accomplish anything positive or productive.

Examples of Low-Value Activities
- Actions and activities that produce a negative outcome for yourself or others
- Watching television for long durations
- Online gaming or playing video games
- Drinking or using substances in excess
- Texting or using social media in excess or when you should be working
- Gossiping with friends or coworkers
- Periods of no or little physical activity

EVALUATION AND SCORING OF ACTIONS

Having given some thought and consideration to the value of our activities, you can now evaluate your regular activities with even more precision. What follows is an easy way to keep score of your actions and choices in order to see where you habitually succeed or fail. This can be conducted through a calendar, or consider using the Balance Me App which will do a lot of the work for you.

Here's how it works. You can earn 0–10 points per hour. It is up to you to determine the score based on the guidelines below. What is most important is that you remain consistent, be honest with yourself, and then actually keep with it. The goal is to monitor when you are engaging in lower-value activities and then begin to replace them with higher-value ones. It is really that simple. Here are some basic guidelines for keeping score. You don't need to overthink the scoring. What is more important is that you are honest and consistent when it comes to tracking your activities.

<u>ACTIVITY VALUE SCALE</u>

10

MULTIPLE GOALS/CATEGORIES ACHIEVEMENT

9

RESULTS OR PROGRESS FOR A GOAL OR CATEGORY

8

POSITIVE GAIN BUT NOT TOWARD YOUR GOALS

7

PRODUCTIVE OUTCOMES FOR LOWER-PRIORITY STUFF

6

MINIMAL PRODUCTIVITY

5

<u>DOWNTIME</u> (SUCH AS COMMUTING)

4

ACTIONS THAT COULD BE IMPROVED

3

VERY LITTLE POSITIVE GAIN

2

NO CHANCE OF PRODUCING POSITIVE GAIN

1

VERY UNPRODUCTIVE

0

RESULTS IN NEGATIVE OUTCOME

Tracking Your Daily and Weekly Actions

Now that you have a basic idea of how the scoring system works, let's talk about putting it into play. For the first several days you will be doing nothing other than tracking and observing your actions. It's okay if you don't create an entry with a corresponding score every hour; however, for maximum impact you will need to account for each hourly block at some point daily. The whole point of doing this is for no other reason than being able to see where we are habitually engaging in low-value activities. Stick with it for at least a week and you will really start to see the large blocks of time where you can easily improve your activities. If you really want to create a stunning visual, find a red, yellow, and green highlighter. In the spots on your calendar scoring 0–3 highlight them in red, 4–7 use the yellow marker, then reserve the green one for scores of 8 or higher.

Action Replacement and Planning

Now that you have identified some high and low activities in your life, you can start using replacement to make changes. This is easy to do and gains fast, effective results. Replacement can be used in many ways. The most powerful is *action replacement*. This is the intentional and deliberate act of replacing an identifiable low-value activity with one that is of higher value. It sounds pretty simple, right? It can be—it's all up to you.

If you are using the calendar system that I just described, you should be able to see where you weren't at your best during the same block of time yesterday or last week, then simply make a plan to do something that moves you toward a goal or creates recognizable balance in your life. Try adding up your total score for a day and comparing it to your score on other days. Or do the same thing for a week and so on. The more you treat it like a game, desiring nothing other than the high score, the more fun it can be.

If you only take one thing from this program, this is the one I recommend. Through the use of action replacement and future planning, you can absolutely change your life faster than through any other method. Think about it for a second. You will not only be eliminating the things that are dragging you down but simultaneously doing things that lift you up. It's a win-win situation. The net positive gain from this approach is above and beyond that of any other method you will find. The greatest part about this approach is that the smallest changes can give you immediate returns!

Now let's take a minute while I bring you the first of multiple conversations I had with successful people from all walks of life. These candid chats offer great insight into finding personal success and balance. My conversations included ones with a rock star, an

Olympic gold medalist, a fashion editor, and a founder of a highly successful franchise. The input they provide is really quite amazing.

A Conversation with
Joel Cummins of Umphrey's McGee

Umphrey's McWho? That might be what you just thought, so let me take a few moments to introduce Joel and the band. Formed in South Bend, Indiana in 1997, Umphrey's McGee has since been performing for live audiences ranging from ten to fifty thousand people. The sextet (six members) consists of Joel Cummins (keyboard/piano), Brendan Bayliss (guitar/vocals) Jake Cinninger (guitar/vocals), Ryan Stasik (bass), Kris Myers (drums), and Andy Farag (percussion).

Umphrey's—or UM as they are commonly called—play improvisation rock 'n' roll. Other bands in this genre are or have been Phish, Grateful Dead, and Widespread Panic. Currently in the genre, many consider UM to have the strongest skills, high versatility, and most creative "jams" out there.

Joel Cummins and his bandmates are not only my musical heroes, but I'm proud to say also my friends. Previously in my career I spent several years working in the music industry—not as a musician but within the music instrument business. During this time, I had the pleasure of meeting a number of interesting individuals but none stood out as much as these guys, especially

Joel who is one of the most positive, friendly, and outwardly caring people I know.

Having spent at least a small amount of time with all or some members of the band each year for the past twelve years, I really noticed something. These guys are not only really freaking good at what they do, but they also work really hard to make sure they bring their fans the very best version of themselves possible each and every night! I'm talking serious dedication when it comes to being the best at what they do.

Okay, that's the backstory of the band. So why and how is this relevant to a well-balanced life? Because since 1997 they have played more than twenty-one hundred shows all over the world. That is roughly one hundred shows *per year*, usually in a different city every night. So I figured Joel would probably have some quality input on the subject.

On August 3, 2016 Umphrey's McGee played a show in my hometown of Kansas City. Prior to their arrival I sent Joel an e-mail and asked if I could talk with him about a "project" I was working on. Still being fairly early in the process of writing the book, I did the best I could to describe the topic, my ideas, and intentions. Much to my delight Joel replied enthusiastically to my e-mail and we set a time to chat before the show.

MATT: With traveling worldwide, what challenges does that present in your personal, professional, and physical life?

JOEL: In regard to maintaining balance in my personal life and the challenges that touring and my schedule provide, I try to limit emotional responses. If you are always rushing then you are probably missing a lot of opportunities, or making careless mistakes.

When it comes to my marriage, my wife also has an interesting schedule, so finding time to spend together can be tough. We precommit to things like trips and vacations to make sure that we schedule them. May and November are months that are usually slower for the band's touring, so Dasha and I will often find time to schedule a vacation during those months. It's really important for us. We try to not go more than a couple of weeks without seeing each other.

For my physical life, I try to get outside more and I practice yoga when and where I can. I've probably had the best balance of my life over the last five years. I try to get exercise at least five days a week. Whenever I travel back home to Venice Beach after a tour, I commit to getting outside and either going for a run or taking a bike ride on the beach. Post travel you can feel very lethargic and oftentimes you need a kick in the butt to get back in gear. Invariably I feel 100 percent more energized once I'm exercising and enjoying some time outdoors after a long travel day.

Are there any indicators that signal imbalance in your life?

I listen to my body; it will tell me when I need sleep. The constant time zone changes and travel present challenges when it comes to resting and sleep. Over the years I have learned to sleep just about anywhere, from tour buses, vans, couches, you name it. But overall getting quality rest is really important. Another important thing is to have some days more planned out and to have some days with more flexibility and openings. Leaning one way too much will either induce stress or leave you without enough of an outline to shape your days.

The adrenaline from performing can also make getting quality rest a challenge. That's why I try and make sure to get sleep or rest in the spots and times when I can. I think taking a nap is something that can be extremely valuable for challenging travel days. It can be twenty minutes, forty-five minutes, but usually not more as that may actually make you *more* tired. But it's a good thing to even take five minutes to close your eyes and relax if you're starting to feel tired. You're not going to be at your best, so why push yourself past that threshold and risk not delivering what you're capable of. On the opposite side of the coin, sometimes as a musician I will play better if I'm tired . . . the edge is gone and there's a certain mindset where you just let things flow more. So one could argue that occasionally performing and being tired is okay!

What would you recommend others do to find balance in their life?

Don't overbook yourself. Have an understanding that often things take longer than you expect them to take. Recognizing that gives you some flexibility and ability to adapt. It's challenging to figure out just what's possible and what's too much. On the same note, don't be lazy. Take chances, do things that you seem "out of the box" for who you think you are. There's so much to learn in the world. And there's a lot that we don't know that we won't even realize we don't know.

Don't be afraid to ask for what you want. And make sure you learn to speak the language of others. Understanding that different people communicate in different ways goes a long way. It's really important to understand that, especially when dealing with creative types. Just because you think you understand someone doesn't mean you should put them in a box and assume you know what they are thinking or how they are going to do something.

How do you control or deal with the positive and negative input? Being someone who does something that gets critiqued on a nightly basis, and in very public forums, how do you deal with the negativity or criticism that some people throw out there?

Take what you do seriously, but not too seriously. Try to stay in the middle. In regard to the criticism . . . we do something that requires taking chances. Sometimes you take that chance and it doesn't come out perfect. You just need to own it, acknowledge it, and then move on. Dwelling on failure is just going to result in more missed opportunity. Sometimes you just have to say yes and go with/for it.

Along the way to any successful destination there is also some doubt. How did you process and deal with it?

In regard to the road leading us to where we are now, we have always tried to have a long-term plan while at the same time satisfying our short-term vision. There are no shortcuts that benefit the long term. I make sure to enjoy my days and what I am doing when I'm doing it. We try to keep our long-term plans and business model reasonable, but at the same time prepared for growth. We have always tried to avoid the short-term payoff that might result in long-term failure.

How do you keep things fresh and/or new? If you have played a song five hundred times how do you keep it enjoyable like it's the fifth time you have played it?

We like taking risks, walking the tightrope. There are moments when no one knows where it is going next and that keeps it new. The way we play pretty much guarantees that it's never the same performance twice. Seeing what people get out of our shows helps. We have really created some great relationships along the way. We have fans that are married and met each other at one of our shows. Just seeing how much enjoyment some of the people in the crowd get out of our shows is amazing. The fact that what we do means a lot to them means a lot to us.

SECTION TWO:

UNDERSTANDING YOUR PERSONALITY AND OTHERS' (DISC)

WHEN I WAS twenty-five years old, like many people that age, I was still trying to find my way in the world. I made the decision to pursue a career in sales and off I went. Having an outgoing personality and a strong desire to earn money I found myself doing well right away; but through my own observations and those of my employer, I knew that I still had a lot to learn. I did really well with certain types of customers but not as well with others. Outgoing people loved me but more introverted types posed a challenge. So in an attempt to self improve I started studying sales. I went to the bookstore and bought an armful of books. I read and then read some more. Each book's process was followed over the following weeks and months. But something was still missing. It was really frustrating. Then one day in yet another trip to the bookstore, I came across *How to Mind-Read Your Customers* by David P. Snyder. Surely this cleverly titled book would reveal some trick or tactic that held the key to my success. So I rushed through the checkout line, got in my car, and immediately headed home to start reading.

I wasn't far into the book when I realized that it didn't in fact tell you how to read someone's mind. After taking a couple minutes to get past that disappointing realization (as how cool would that be?), I continued reading. What I then learned changed my life, and I am not kidding one bit. Snyder clearly laid out the solution to all of my problems on the sales floor. How? By introducing me to DiSC and then explaining how it was relevant to my situation.

So what is DiSC? It is a way of assessing someone's personality traits by placing us in one of four underlying categories: Dominant, Influential, Steadfast, and Conscientious. You might guess which one you are from those names alone.

Using DiSC I learned how my own personality style was viewed by others. I discovered many of my own strengths, but more importantly what my weakness were likely to be.

So how does this apply to having a well-balanced life? Well that is pretty easy. Understanding your strengths and weaknesses is beneficial in all areas of your life. By understanding how your personality style interacts with others, you can learn to have healthier and more productive relationships. This benefits you in your personal and professional life first, but it also deflects the negative results from impacting your physical life. By reducing the frustration, anxiety, and negativity that is produced when poor relationships are present, you in turn make your life more balanced. The product of poor relationships is heavy. We then have to carry it around with us and the result is more feelings of anxiety or negativity. A lot of people don't pay attention to their own weaknesses because it is easier to avoid the subject. Don't be one of those people. As uncomfortable as it might feel to understand your weaknesses or undesirable traits, doing so is paramount when it comes to finding success and balance in your life.

When people talk about strengths versus weaknesses, they don't really give any consideration to the fact that around our strengths hover and orbit our weaknesses. I'll use myself as an example. Often times I have a tendency to talk too much. I can be loud and wander off subject. While these are not my *desired* personality traits, my doing this has a lot to do with my being someone who feels like he has a lot to say. The "strength" part of this is in the form of fearlessness when it comes to public speaking or presenting. I feel very comfortable presenting products or programs in front of any number of people. The "weakness" part is that I can come across in one-on-one or group situations as a little too controlling of the conversation, possibly rubbing people the wrong way. So there it was! My customers with different personality styles weren't hearing what I was trying to say because of . . . ME!

Over the next several months and what then became years, I continued learning about personality styles and how people with different or even similar ones interacted. I quickly realized that this understanding helped me get what I wanted more often. Now when I say that, it's not in a tricky way. There's no actual mind reading. I simply learned how to better deliver my message in a way that people who weren't exactly like me would want to hear it. I also learned how to be mindful about certain messages I was unknowingly sending with my body language. That being said, I am a big guy with an even bigger voice. Some people can handle that, others can't. So being able to identify that helped me tone down certain tendencies, thus delivering my message more effectively.

Let's be more specific about how understanding my own personality and that of others helped me. Improved communication helped me reduce stressful relationships in the workplace and in my personal life, which meant I encountered a whole lot less stress and stressful situations. I came to understand that it is easier to exist when you aren't just thinking about YOU and instead consider EVERYONE around you. I learned that certain people want to hear about every single detail while others don't care at all. I truly changed my thought process and actions by just making a few simple changes. The changes I needed to make were almost all when dealing with more introverted types. My large stature coupled with an excited and sometimes loud voice was more or less freaking some people out. While not vocalizing it they saw me as moving too fast, possibly making decisions without thought, and in some situations a bit intimidating. So I slowed down with those types; I made sure I wasn't being imposing and, more importantly, I made sure I was listening patiently.

Now the strengths in one area of your life may not carry over to other areas of your life. An example: as a business owner, you have control over your business and make daily decisions that impact the direction of the company. Yet when vacationing with the family you prefer to relax and let others plan the vacation so you can enjoy your time. In this case, your strength of decision-making in your business doesn't carry over to the vacation, but that's by choice. While weaknesses can have a negative connotation, they should be thought of as areas where you can improve. Or you can also acknowledge that a weakness in a particular area may not really be relevant to your goals—and that's okay. They don't have to be.

What seems like a strength to one person might not necessarily seem that useful to others. This is where stress and then feelings of imbalance occur. Being able to understand yourself first allows you to adapt your personality when dealing with other personalities.

PERSONALITY SELF-ASSESSMENT - DiSC

Here is some in-depth information, history, and practical application of DiSC. We all have personalities that fall into four general categories:

1. *Dominant* (direct, strong-willed, and forceful)
2. *Influential* (sociable, talkative, and lively)
3. *Steadfast* (gentle, accommodating, and softhearted)
4. *Conscientious* (private, analytical, and logical), sometimes called *Compliant*

DiSC was first developed in the 1920s by William Marston, who studied how people's sense of self and their interaction with their environment were directly related to their behavioral traits. He was interested in using practical explanations to help people understand and manage their experiences and relationships. Over the years, others in the field updated and developed more advanced versions that are frequently used by businesses to help build functional teams, evaluate potential employees' abilities to fit into existing teams, and a whole lot of other uses related to the workplace.

So how does the evaluation work? Most tools that use the DiSC method to evaluate your personality style do so by proposing qualities or scenarios and then gauging how much you personally agree or disagree.

Examples:

Sometimes I really feel the need to make my opinion heard.

Meeting and talking to new people is easy for me.

People usually find me to be a good listener.

I think it is important to be accurate when I make statements.

Then depending on the version of the evaluation you are taking (there are several companies that offer them), you generally pick the statement that is most like you, then the one that is least like you. Some evaluations might ask you to take four to five statements and rank them according to which is most or least like you. The bottom line is that they all evaluate you on how you view yourself. You might be thinking, *Wait, I thought this was about how* others *see me?!* It is, but how others see you is a direct result of *how you see yourself.* So let's nerd out a little on the science of personality styles.

NATURAL AND ADAPTED PERSONALITY STYLES

Before we get into the specifics of each personality style it is important to know that we can have very different personality styles in different situations. The styles are known as *natural* and *adapted.*

Your natural personality style is most commonly accessed in your personal life. This is where you most often feel free being YOU. You feel a lot more comfortable when you are around friends or family, or you possibly don't feel like you need to act a specific way, such as the image you might try and project to others at work.

Your adapted personality traits are accessed when you leave your natural surroundings and are placed in situations such as work. You might also access these traits when you are out in public or involved with groups of people and want to project a certain image.

Another important part of understanding your personality style and how it relates to others is that whether you are exhibiting your natural or adapted personality style, you will always show your least desirable traits when you are stressed or under pressure. Through describing the different personality styles, I will list what some of those negative traits are. This understanding can help you prevent damaging your relationships with others and also are a signal that you might need to assess and reevaluate your situation.

Here's a more detailed look at the four styles of personalities—what their strengths and weaknesses are, the goals they typically have, some areas where they could improve, and the best way to communicate with each. Pay particular attention to whichever resonates with you.

Dominant Personality (D Style)

If you have a D personality style you have probably been referred to as a "type A" person. When addressing others, you are most likely direct and decisive, which can sometimes be an issue as some people take such delivery the wrong way. Most of the time you are a leader and like to take charge of the situation. Your strong-willed, driven, and determined demeanor causes others to see and describe you as confident—possibly even "cocky" or arrogant. You are likely a self-starter and a problem solver who others look to for decisions and direction. Your ability to look at the big picture, place tremendous value on time frames, and demand to see immediate results makes you an ideal candidate for business and entrepreneurship. New challenges, love of winning, competing, and succeeding are likely to be motivators for you.

Because your personality style likes to see quick results, you may bite off a bit more than you can chew when it comes to tasks, jobs, or projects. Routine, mundane, and repetitive tasks not only bore you but can make you *totally* frustrated. When it comes to your personal and professional life, you're often perceived as not listening to others. This comes from your natural desire to be in control. That coupled with your direct nature means that you might need to work harder to develop your personal relationships by becoming friendlier and more approachable.

You want others to be direct, to the point, and brief. If they bring you a problem, you prefer that they be ready with possible solutions, getting right to the point. You love innovative and progressive ideas, but need someone else to work out the details and specifics.

Does this sound like you? It pretty much describes me down to the last detail. So when it comes to the Type D personality, I am a bit of an expert. I can attest firsthand to some of the benefits and challenges this personality type brings with it. However if you can reign in the volatile elements of your personality and channel them in a positive direction then I feel bad for your competition. It took me YEARS to figure that out, but the payoff was substantial. Here are a few more details about your personality type that you might find interesting. Remember, it is just as important to understand the personality styles of others as it is your own. So if you aren't a Type D then use this information to better understand the Type D's in your life.

Positive Traits
Direct and decisive
Prefers to lead than follow
Likes leadership and management roles
High self-confidence
Risk-taker
Problem solver
Self-starter

Negative Traits
Oversteps authority, prefers to be in charge
Can be argumentative and not listen to the reasoning of others
Doesn't like repetition and routine
Ignores details of a situation, even if they're important
Attempts to do too much at one time, hoping to see quick results
Can be intimidating when working in groups
Overly direct, blunt
Lack of social interest around others
Can be demanding and insensitive
Cannot let things be, controlling

Best Way to Communicate with a D Style Personality
Be direct, to the point, and brief
Focus on business instead of social topics

Try to be results-oriented
Focus on the solution, not the problem

Traits in Natural or Adapted Settings
Focuses on the future and big picture
Enjoys nonroutine challenging tasks and activities
Motivated by projects that produce physical, trackable,
or tangible results
Functions well with heavy workloads and when under
stress
Welcomes new challenges and risks without fear

Common Goals
Unique accomplishments
New opportunities
Control of audience
Independence

Employment Trends
CEO
Entrepreneur
Business owner
Manager
Jobs that use leadership skills
Lobbyist
Principal
Sales
Announcer

INFLUENTIAL PERSONALITY (I STYLE)

At first the Type D and Type I personalities can resemble each other. After all they both exist in the world of extroverts, or the outgoing. If you love being the center of attention, you're most likely a Type I personality. You are a "type A" person far more than the D personality. You're enthusiastic, optimistic, talkative, persuasive, impulsive, and emotional. Your ability to influence and inspire others makes you very popular in most settings, which lead to you functioning at your best when you're around people and working with groups. Others most likely see you as a creative problem solver who can think "outside the box." Enjoying the role of "coach" you find yourself encouraging and motivating those around you. You can't get enough action, but at the same time really don't like conflict among those in your group. In fact you go out of your way to prevent it.

It's likely that a lack of organization, attention to details, and follow-through haunt you in your personal and professional life. You're so busy being the talker or presenter that you need—and prefer—for someone else to handle the details. You have the confidence to make decisions, but probably often do so impulsively. Because you're such a quick thinker, it would be helpful for you to slow down a bit, focusing on listening rather than talking. This will help you keep track of the particulars of the situation and also force you to think things through.

When others are communicating with you the preference is that they don't overload you with details. If you are communicating with a Type I person it is best to get to the point, then allow them to respond without interruption. While this personality type is typically "chatty," that characteristic is often how they arrive at their best ideas and solutions, so consider letting them just talk it out.

If you are a Type I, or you deal with one regularly, it is important to remember that they are emotional. Much like we have discussed already, our strengths and weaknesses live next door to each other. This emotional quality can fuel huge amounts of success or failure. This is where the balancing act exists. It is important to take advantage of the positive traits when present and to immediately try and curb or limit the negative qualities they surface. This basic approach is likely to lead to "hot streaks" of positive outcomes and also will prevent moments that can or could be considered self-destructive.

Positive Traits
Not afraid to be the center of attention
Enthusiastic
Optimistic
Talkative
Functions best when around people and working in teams
Creative problem solvers who can think outside the box
Encourages and motivates others

63

Avoids conflict and keeps the peace

Negative Traits
Not good with details
Impulsive and emotional
More concerned with people and popularity than with tangible results and organization
Poor listeners
Can talk too much in some settings

Best Ways to Communicate with an I Style Personality
Flatter and praise them
Build rapport
Provide a friendly and fun environment
Don't eliminate social time—they're very motivated by this
Don't do all the talking or strictly tell them what to do—you'll miss the opportunity to hear their ideas and creative solutions to problems

Traits in a Natural or Adapted Setting
They're impulsive decision-makers and would benefit from doing research before acting
They're wonderful at presenting, motivating, and problem-solving, but sometimes slow to action
They're quick thinkers and need to slow down the pace when in teams

Common Goals
Victory with flair

Friendship and happiness
Authority and prestige
Becoming status symbols
Popularity

Employment Trends
Training representative
Arbitrator
Advertising manager
Office manager
Spokesperson
Sales

STEADFAST PERSONALITY (S STYLE)

Are you known for being stable, predictable, patient, and consistent? Do people refer to you as a "type B" personality or an introvert rather than an extrovert? If this is you then you are most likely a Type S, a steadfast personality. This means you listen well and love working with others. You're dependable and compliant toward authority and a loyal team player. Multitasking is a strength as well as following tasks through to completion. In fact it probably bothers you when something isn't complete. In your professional life procedures and systems being in place is important for you.

Your natural common sense allows you to see a simpler or more practical way to accomplish goals.

Seeing the "big picture" is easy for you as well as understanding the steps needed to get there. The idea of setting a goal and creating a plan is a "no-brainer" for you. This makes you an excellent coworker and team member in many professional settings.

You love your routines and stick with them, so you can be perceived as fearing change, which leads to indecisiveness. If change is needed you can handle it, but prefer to have time to adjust. Saying "no" isn't always easy for you, as you do like to please. Your attention to detail can result in your working at a slower and more systematic pace. Be aware that this can lead to the perception that you are slowing down progress.

When people communicate with you your preference is for them to be friendly, expressing their interest in you as well as the information. If you are not a Type S and are communicating with one make sure you take time to provide clarification if necessary. Always be polite and avoid being confrontational, overly aggressive, or rude toward Type S personality types. Not doing so can lead to a lengthy time frame when it comes to restoring the relationship to full strength.

As a Type S personality, asking for what you want is sometimes a challenge. Therefore, it is crucial that you force yourself to do so. This will help you escape from situations or limitations that you are more or less imposing on yourself by NOT doing so. You might find it helpful to actually practice asking when in a private setting. Yes, that is right; I want you to talk to yourself when no one is around. It will make it that much easier to "go for it" once you have already spoken the words several times.

Positive Traits
Steady, stable, and predictable
Even-tempered, friendly
Sympathetic and generous
Understanding, patient listeners
Reliable and dependable
Want to work in a harmonious way
Compliant toward authority
Team player

Negative Traits
Opposition toward change
Can hold grudges
Easily frustrated and resentful instead of facing issues head on
Sensitive toward criticism
Likes to please others so has a hard time saying no or establishing priorities

Best Ways to Communicate with an S Style Personality
Be personable and build rapport
Be patient and kind
Avoid being confrontational, overly aggressive, pushy, or demanding

When they feel comfortable around you, they will open up

Traits in a Natural or Adapted Setting
Flourishes in a team setting especially in groups that they trust and feel comfortable around
Likes environments with little change or surprise and no conflict
Likes to complete tasks from beginning to end
Likes procedures and systems

Common Goals
Personal accomplishments
Group acceptance
Power through formal roles and positions of authority
Maintenance of status quo and controlled environment

Employment Trends
Investigator
Pharmacist
Counselor
Market research analyst
Programmer
Lab technician

Conscientious Personality (C Style)

Are you accurate, precise, detail oriented, careful, diplomatic, and conscientious? Do you think through every detail and process of how something works? If so you are likely a Type C personality. You have certainly been referred as an introvert or "type B" person. You are the "research scientist" of personality types, striving for consistency and accuracy. You also take a lot of pride in the quality of your work. Since you are a great problem solver you can see what others don't. This is due to your ability to focus on details more than any other personality types can. The downside of this is that because you pay such attention to details, it's sometimes difficult for you to see the big picture.

In your personal and professional life your attention to detail can lead to you being critical toward others who aren't. Even though you fear criticism, you can tend to be overly critical of others. You enjoy clear-cut boundaries and work best in a peaceful and organized environment. Preferring to work alone, you aren't particularly motivated by the social settings at work.

When communicating with Type C personalities make sure to give all of the details and to keep them well-informed. If you are a Type D or Type I personality it is best to tone down those qualities, as they are NOT working in your favor. If you are a type C personality and communicating with a D or I type, it is important that you shorten the delivery of your message and if possible just get right to the point.

As a Type C personality vocalizing your needs, opinions, or issues isn't going to be your strong suit. If you want to achieve a balanced life you are going to need to recognize this and work to overcome it. Not doing so is likely to lead to a lot of anxiety and stress, mainly because you are keeping it all bottled up. While "verbal" communication might not be your preference, that's okay, communication can come in all forms in this day and age. Just make sure to get it out! Internalizing the issue won't help in the long run.

Positive Traits
Accurate
Precise
Detail oriented
Makes decisions with plenty of research and information to back it up
Sets high standards for themselves and others
Tend to be good problem solvers
Creative because of focusing on the details and seeing what others don't

Negative Traits
Avoids conflict rather than arguing
Difficulty verbalizing their feelings
Needs clear-cut boundaries to feel comfortable
Can get caught up in the details, leading to a lack of seeing the bigger picture

Best Way to Communicate with the C Personality Style
Be patient, persistent, and diplomatic—they fear criticism

Try not to answer questions too vaguely because they need information and details to make sense of new plans and decisions

If you criticize, be specific with your examples and be diplomatic

Being confrontational makes them not respond well and close off

Traits in a Natural or Adapted Setting
Loves an environment that is peaceful and organized with little to no conflicts or arguments

They don't need to work with or be around people and tend to be loners

They feel safest when there are procedures and routines and they know what's expected of them

Common Goals
Correctness
Stability
Predictable accomplishments
Personal growth

Employment Trends
Medical record technician
Accountant
Job analyst
Caseworker
Historian
Pilot
Architect

Practical Application of DiSC

When and how do you use this information? Probably the first thing you did as you read through the four personality types was to identify yourself. More than likely, you also identified people you know who fit into each of the categories. A strong understanding of who you are and the way that you are perceived by others lends a meaningful advantage when it comes to forming and maintaining strong and productive relationships in your personal and professional life.

Perception is reality. Have you heard this before? This is something I want you to really think about going forward. Let me explain. Each of us has, on some level, our own reality. It exists within and around ourselves. Therefore, if your actions or personality lead another person to think of you in a positive or negative way, then on some level it is reality. So if you are having a bad day and you let your negative personality traits show and a coworker thinks you are a jerk, then in that person's reality, you are. Understanding this concept will enhance your ability to understand why others might react to you the way that they do. That being said, no matter how hard you try, you aren't going to please everyone. In fact, you shouldn't try to. But on a smaller scale when you give consideration to how you might be viewed by others you can then form a better plan, or at least a more thoughtful one when it comes to future interactions.

Personality Styles and Your Personal Life

In your personal life— social situations—similar personalities tend to seek each other out, which is particularly true with the influential, steadfast, and conscientious types. For the influential types, the more, the merrier—bring on the people and lots of them! The steadfast and conscientious types are more inward-focused and may share some of the same activities. The dominant styles will hang together for a while, but they're so competitive that it's not as enjoyable for them. They see the influential style as people who just want to have fun, and consider the steadfast and conscientious types as boring. But these personality types can learn from each other when interacting socially. The dominant can become more patient and responsive when around the steadfast and conscientious personalities. Conversely, the steadfast can draw on the dominant's style for taking risks. The influential can learn a little indiscretion from the steadfast and conscientious. And those two personalities can relax and be allowed to be drawn out of their shell by the influential.

Personal Category in Action

David is a D personality; in fact, he almost pegs the graph when taking a personality inventory. He owns his own business and is used to being in charge. In his personal life his natural style is still that of a D. David's son is involved in Cub Scouts. At the end of each pack meeting the group and parents discuss future activities with Scott, the pack leader. During these sessions David regularly and firmly suggests what the group should do going forward and where it should occur. Scott is a Type C personality. He listens to suggestions and diligently researches them. Because Scott and David have different personality styles, Scott sees David as being a little pushy and somewhat arrogant. This leads to a bit of a tension between the two as David sees Scott as being too patient and unwilling to make a decision about their activities.

So what is a good way for each to effectively communicate with the other?

David is more likely to effectively converse with Scott if he is able to appeal to the communication methods that Scott responds to more favorably. The same goes back the other way. David would be best to present his ideas in a more structured manner, doing so at a time that Scott might feel is appropriate. David needs to support his opinions with facts or supporting information that gives more validity to his opinions.

When communicating with David, Scott would get the best results by being direct. David is less concerned with the long list of supporting data and would respond more favorably if simply given the possible options right away, and then if he chooses to inquire about additional information, he will ask for it.

Neither Scott nor David is right or wrong. However, through a stronger understanding of how each other can, could, or will respond to the other's personality styles, each would be able to achieve more effective and productive communication.

Personality Styles and Your Professional Life

Now let's bring it back to business. When it comes to the professional area of your life, the dynamics of personalities change dramatically. A business might be running like a well-oiled machine, but when personality styles aren't working together, conflicts arise and inefficiencies develop. Personality differences—which determine the way we approach tasks and how we react to others—are usually the primary triggers of conflict. Encountering someone who doesn't share the same approach you take can be extremely frustrating. This is where knowing your personality type and that of those around you can help resolve conflicts and adapt your compatibility. By knowing what each of the personality types brings to the table, conflicts can be resolved and a more harmonious and productive environment created.

PROFESSIONAL CATEGORY IN ACTION

Let's imagine that a dominant business owner hires an accountant who is also a dominant style. This combination is one of the least compatible because they inherently see each other as competitors; both like control, work quickly, and have no need for details. Expect major clashes! For the accountant, this doesn't work so well, given the accuracy and detailed nature of the position.

If, on the other hand, the accountant's personality style is *conscientious*, the work performed will be what the dominant business owner seeks. However, each will need to be aware of and work on their communication with each other. The business owner will need to learn to attack the issue, not the person, while the accountant will need to learn to be direct, skipping details and just giving an overview of facts. The steady style of a conscientious personality tends to get along with everyone. They thrive on harmony and thus enjoy making contributions and being productive in their work environment. As long as the dominant business owner focuses on compromise and working together to find common ground, these two personalities will get along.

Now if this business owner hires an *influential* personality, there's some work both are going to have to do for compatibility on the job. Socially they'll get along great because of shared outgoing personalities. They both like control, tend to focus on the big picture, and don't like messing with the details. Approaching the influential type in a positive, nonconfrontational way with a sense of humor goes a long way in resolving conflicts.

Now that you have a better understanding of personality styles through the use of DiSC, it's time to start using it. Remember, through healthier and more productive relationships with those around us the chance of feeling balance and accomplishing our goals is that much greater. Practical application of this information requires continual review in order to make it part of your regular thought process. As we continue on to the next section of *Balance Me* consider how this understanding of others can be used as a solution to some of the common issues in your life. I think you will be surprised at how quickly you see results!

A Conversation with
Olympic Gold Medalist
Christie Ambrosi

Christie Ambrosi is easily the best athlete I have ever known. She is a four-time NCAA All-American, NCAA National Champion, and a Gold Medalist in Softball from the 2000 Olympic Games in Sydney. Wow! Right? She and I went to high school together. In high school I played on the baseball team. Since the baseball and softball team shared some of the same facilities I got a first-hand experience with the level of dedication and amount of work Christie put in to be prepared for the later opportunities she would have in her sport. On a personal level she is one of the more inspiring and positive people I have ever known.

MATT: During your days as an athlete did you consider that a professional thing? Or was it more personal?

CHRISTIE: It was fun; it was more personal. I felt it was more like an escape because I had a lot going on in my personal life. It was the fun part of my life at that time.

Starting in your youth and progressing into college and after, what were some of the challenges you had in regard to finding balance and did you do anything specific to deal with them?

When I was in college, I was in such a routine. I'm a worker—if my coach tells me to do it, I do it. If I was told when to be in classes or when to be at practice, I was there. I wanted to win. My ultimate goal was to win. I surround myself with people who are like that. One of the things my coach in college said is there's the 33% Rule: 33% of the people you meet will suck the life out of you. They're negative, they're "Debbie Downers." The middle third depends on whom they are standing next to—they don't really have a backbone. The top third is positive, overachievers, they see the glass as half full, they're leaders, and that's the kind of people I surround myself with. I'm not saying I'm always up there; I'm not perfect. If I'm negative, I remind myself that I'm being a bottom third and I don't want to be in the bottom third.

What triggers that?

Self-awareness. One thing I was so blessed with was to be surrounded by coaches who coached me and the life lessons they taught me. Being accountable and responsible and being able to own up to your mistakes was one of the best, but hardest things to learn. You never want to admit you were wrong. It's hard to say you're sorry. It's gotten a lot easier as I got older but it's not been easy to get here.

Athletes and entrepreneurs are closely aligned. There's that personality style that likes winning. You can't fear failure. How do you overcome it when you get to a world stage like the Olympics?

You have to be a leaper. Sometimes you're going to jump off the cliff and fall flat on your face but it's worth the risk. When you jump and everything works out it's the most gratifying feeling in the world. In the sport of softball, you fail more than you succeed, so it teaches you how to deal with failure. If you're going to be successful, you have to know how to fail. You have to have a short-term memory. You have to pick yourself up and move on quickly. And that's not easy.

As an athlete you get subjected to criticism—you should have done it this way, or that way. You failed when we needed you to succeed. How did you deal with that?

I never got that. I really wasn't subjected to that, but if I was, I don't know if I could have handled it that well.

If you were talking to a younger version of you—someone who is fifteen or sixteen who is showing a high level of talent in sports, how would you tell them to handle it?

You don't have to tell those kids a lot—they get it. You're born with that "want to." You can't make somebody want something. I love softball, and when I love something, I give everything to it. I can tell when somebody loves softball, but if they don't, I can't make them love it. You try to make it fun so that they fall in love with it. There's a balance with having fun and working hard. This generation is lazy and doesn't have good work ethics. We tend to think there's more talent because there are more facilities, more instruction, more technology, and more athletes giving back to the sport. Kids feel an entitlement to everything including being good in sports. And that's never going to change. That's old school. No technology will ever change the fact that you have to work hard at it to be good at it.

When you were growing up, did you ever have goals—especially written goals?

Yes! When I was a freshman my coach asked us to write down our goals. Mine was to go play at UCLA or Arizona, and then go to the Olympics. After I got back from the Olympics there was a ceremony in downtown Overland Park for me, and my coach had kept my written goals and gave them back to me.

SECTION THREE:

ALL THINGS MARRIAGE AND FAMILY

FAMILY IS EVERYTHING! It can be our greatest source of joy or deepest cause of sorrow. And it's very often our strongest motivating factor. Our partner or spouse, children, parents, and siblings are the people we're closest to in life. The health of familial relationships can have the biggest impact when it comes to whether or not our life feels balanced.

Let's say you have an eight-year-old child in third grade. You get a call from the teacher telling you that your child was sent to the principal's office due to poor behavior. The call comes in at 1:00 p.m. on a weekday while you are at work. This personal situation will now have a direct impact on your professional life. As a result of your child's poor behavior, you have to now leave work to pick up your child.

There are also a lot of other ways relationships in your family can have an impact on your professional or physical being. Let's take a situation that might be a little less comfortable to talk about. Let's say the same eight-year-old child is suffering from a health issue that requires frequent visits to the doctor that are expensive, stressful, and time-consuming. A situation like that can consume your focus because your child's well-being is more important than other things in your life. So now this stress can have an effect on your physical being, contributing to a lack of sleep, which then leads to difficulty concentrating on your work. You fall behind, or maybe you're not paying as close attention to your business and things start to wobble. There are things that you're going to be able to control and there are things that you can't, so being able to have some kind of realization and grasp on what you can and can't control is probably something that's going to help you manage the situation.

Family relationships and their input—or lack thereof—deeply influence who we become, what we accept as success or failure, our character, our beliefs, our opinions, and the decisions big and small we make each and every day. I'm going to spend a fair amount of time discussing marriage, family, and children because having a healthy and productive home life clears the path to success in *all* three P's. On the flip side, a poor marital or home life will make the feeling of balance nearly impossible.

MARRIAGE

People say a lot of different and often contradictory things about marriage; it is amazing, stressful, beautiful, and other stuff I might not want to publish. Opinions about the institution vary when you speak to people of different ages—likely a reflection of the changing expectations and realities that married people find in their lives. Over the course of my lifetime, which began in 1975, the number of people getting married has fallen dramatically. And presently, when asked, just over 60 percent of men and women classify their marriages as "very happy."[2] I hate to sound like a downer, but if you get married today it's a coin toss as to whether you and your spouse will make it as partners.

But why?

Well there are a lot of answers to the *why* part of marriage statistics. In fact, *a whole lot* of reasons. These are the most common sources of stress and negativity in marriages:

1. Financial issues
2. Poor communication
3. Family issues
4. Sexual problems
5. Friends
6. Addictions
7. Physical or verbal abuse
8. Personality differences
9. Unmet or unreal expectations
10. Poor time management

Now that we have a basic understanding of potential stressors in a marriage, let's delve deeper and proactively discuss some solutions.

HOW TO REDUCE FINANCIAL STRESS IN A MARRIAGE

---

[2] Kamp Dush, C. M., Taylor, M. G. and Kroeger, R. A. (2008), Marital Happiness and Psychological Well-Being Across the Life Course*. Family Relations, 57: 211-226. Doi:10.1111/j.1741-3729.2008.00495.x

Money is most often the number one cause of stress within marriages. This can come in many forms. Affected couples fail to adequately communicate to the other about their current financial situation. It might start with the lack of a realistic budget or long-term financial plan, ongoing debt, or just not seeing eye to eye about how, where, when, or which existing funds should be used. Lack of open communication about your finances can easily lead to a trip to divorce court, which by the way only makes financial matters worse.

So what are some easy ways to communicate about finance in your marriage?

- Schedule a regular time to discuss bills, debts, or your family budget. Be accountable.
- Create a mutually agreeable budget or plan at your meeting then STICK TO IT!
- Make a plan that takes care of both the present and the future. More specifically, aggressively pay down debt while at the same time reasonably provide for yourself.
- Set reasonable expectations for each other's spending.

AND DON'T DO ANYTHING TO MAKE IT WORSE! NO NEW DEBT!

One thing I've always recommended is to treat your life like a business, which forces us to have financial restraint. It also forces to make decisions that are based less on emotion and more on common sense and that's not always easy to do. How can you *not* make an emotional decision about your spouse, your child, or your life? All I am trying to say is that you need to consider a more business-like approach. At your business, if you keep writing checks but don't have the cash you'll eventually go out of business. Your personal life is the same way.

IMPROVING MARITAL COMMUNICATION

Let's start by acknowledging that men and women can communicate differently. Yes, I know, we can't generalize the whole male/female population in one sentence, however I'm going to at least try. The intrinsic nature of men is often that of aggressive problem-solving (HIM: "Well if you would just STOP doing this and instead do THIS!"). Many women utilize a more nurturing approach (HER: "Ah, honey, I'm sorry that you had a tough time with that. I wouldn't have liked that at all."). Did I at least come close here? Well, if it applies to your partner, try taking an approach that is more in line with *their* natural response the next time something potentially divisive comes up. The effort will go a long way. It might feel really foreign the first time, but after you see the positive results you're likely to feel *very* comfortable with it.

Another important thing to remember is that your partner is NOT a mind reader! It is an unfair expectation that he or she should know and understand what is bothering you without you first expressing your feelings. Try this logical approach: "There is something I need to talk about with you. It has really been bothering me and I would like to talk with you about it so we can figure something out." Be prepared to have a non-emotionally charged discussion too. Getting overly vocal, animated, or making a lot of accusations right away isn't going to help. In fact, it's going to remove any possibility of having a rational discussion. Calm is key—especially when you are telling someone stuff that isn't favorable. Being as calm as possible will create a mood that is far more receptive and productive. Otherwise you're only opening the door to confrontation and more disagreement!

Remember: *If you are going to bring up a problem, it is best to have some possible solutions too!*

Why Does My Mother-in-Law Hate Me?

That is a loaded question and in some situations might require publication of an additional book to answer. When you get married you are in many ways also marrying your partner's family. By this I mean you are near-guaranteed continued interaction with your partner's father, mother, siblings, cousins, and friends. From this you will be party to a new set of outside opinions, expectations, and sometimes drama.

So what now? Start with the understanding that your "new" family members are people you will see regularly for years to come. Knowing this, is it really a good idea to do things to deteriorate the relationship? I shouldn't need to answer that for you, so I won't. Maybe you are fortunate in that your in-laws are great people who respect boundaries and you sincerely enjoy their company. But if you *aren't* in that situation it is time to consider that you should probably do your best to make the most of the situation. Arguing, criticizing, ignoring, or acting poorly toward your partner's relatives—deserved or not—is just going to create difficult situations for you in the haven of your own home. Never put your spouse in the middle. As my own father used to say, "Sometimes you have to do things you don't want to do. It's part of life."

"Do You Still Think I Am Attractive?"

Though possibly phrased differently when spoken by men or women, it invariably is what we can all begin to wonder when our sex lives fizzle. Couples with young children run into this A LOT. I'm not going to spend much time here, as I prefer to avoid the topics of sex, religion, and politics. What I will say is that we all want to feel wanted. If your love life at home seems to be stalling out, consider that there are a lot of different components involved. It's important to show and tell your partner that you love them. It's also meaningful to reassure them beyond the issue of physical intimacy. Basically confirming that no one is being taken for granted really goes a long way. It is easy to forget to do all of this stuff. Fortunately it is just as easy to start doing it again. There are a whole lot of books, information, and other stuff out there to help. Whatever you and your partner are both comfortable with is likely to help.

Should Your Friends Be My Friends Too?

That is a tough question. It warrants a closer examination of what kind of input these friends provide, what amount of time you want to spend with them, and also what situations do you find yourself in when with them. A GOOD friend will do their best to never come between you and your partner. If friends are negative in regard to your marriage it can be toxic. Consider this: Some friends might make negative statements about your marriage because they are actually jealous. Other friends might also not be as great as you think they are. What is important to remember is that you aren't married to your friends.

Your family should always come first, then friends. Having separate friends is fine. After all you did both have a life prior to becoming a couple, but try and be mindful about the balance that needs to exist between both. One last thing to consider is that just because they are your friends doesn't automatically require your partner to spend time with them, meaning if your partner doesn't seem to enjoy spending time with your friends then don't make them do it. This continues to demonstrate that it is okay for each of you to have a life that isn't codependent on the other.

Addictions, Bad Habits, and Trying to Force Change

Let me start by saying that it is nearly impossible to make someone change unless they *want* to change. If your partner or both of you have addictions or bad habits then your ship is headed toward the rocks. Beware! Drugs, alcohol, gambling, sex, overspending . . . we can go on and on. So what can you do? That is a complex question. It starts with determining whether or not that person understands and acknowledges that a problem exists. In many situations only one of you will believe the other has a problem. The way I look at, if your actions are causing problems for your partner then you *do* in fact have a problem. Remember, perception is reality, so if in the eyes of your partner your actions are problematic, then you do in fact on some level have something to address.

I don't want to sound insensitive toward addiction but when reduced to its lowest common denominator you either choose to do something or not do something. Addiction is psychological or physical with the affected person often unable to control the situation regardless of the wish to do so. A truly addicted person feels driven, compelled, and controlled by it. Physical addiction can lead the affected to engage in activities or decisions that are so far from normative behavior that you might think a stranger was in front of you. Psychological addictions can be equally compelling, and in some ways they too have a physical element with the affected only gaining satisfaction from the feeling that results from the addiction. If you or your partner has a physical or psychological addiction, it is best addressed with a qualified professional who specializes in treating addictions.

Habits, on the other hand, are far easier to change or gain control of. You can use something as simple as replacement to try and create change right away. Or simply STOP doing it each time you recognize the presence of unwanted action. It can take a fair amount of repetition to form a new, positive habit, but correcting bad habits is something well within your grasp *if you want it to be.*

I began this section by stating that you can't expect to force change on another person. While your displeasure with the act can be a motivating factor in the person's decision to change, in the end if they don't want to change, they probably won't. This is really, really tough to accept, especially when it comes to loved ones. For many of us it is natural to try to fix someone as we are used to fixing other stuff in our life. But in regard to others, you need to take a different approach. Start by trying to calmly discuss the issue. Explain the impact the unwanted actions are having on their life— and yours. Express love and support by telling them that you DO care and want to help. Offer to assist finding the aid they may need. Expect to fail and fail and maybe fail again. But if you love and care for someone understand that some forms of addiction and even bad habits require time to fix. At the same time, you also will need to be reasonable and true to yourself. If you are in a situation that is endangering yourself or your children, then your level of understanding should be minimal if even existing at all. Find safety and *then* choose a course of action. Just remember, it is up to you to decide what is best for you and whether or not you believe others are able to or committed to real change.

NEVER ACCEPT ABUSE

If someone loves you and cares, then they won't abuse you. Period. Regardless of what they say, it is not your fault. There are NO situations where physical or verbal abuse is acceptable. Whether it is directed at you or your children it is WRONG 100 percent of the time. I cannot and will not tell you that this situation is salvageable. I have zero tolerance or respect for those who feel it is okay to physically or verbally abuse others. Therefore, I cannot in good conscience tell you I believe there are ways to fix the situation.

People who engage in abusive behavior are HIGHLY likely to do it again. If you feel trapped in an abusive situation, then I BEG you to try and do whatever it takes to get out. Yes, it is normal to feel scared and helpless, however there are people who can and will help you. Start with members of your family. If that isn't possible, there are lots of organizations, groups, and programs that can help. Again, it is never your fault, you should never accept it, and regardless of what the abuser says, they are unlikely to change. You can have a better life, but you will have to start by taking control and leaving the situation.

National Domestic Violence Hotline: 1-800-799-7233

Why Aren't You More Like Me?

Does your personality complement or conflict with your partner's? Sometimes two people who are highly similar to each other will end up in a situation that leads to problems, and other times people who are exact opposites have harmonious and lasting relationships. As you learned earlier, we each exhibit different personality types and some have a tendency to conflict with each other. By understanding and learning more about your partner's personality type and what approach they find the most favorable, you can quickly and easily improve your marriage. For instance, being a Type D, a dominant personality, I have to tone down parts of my personality in order to communicate more effectively with my wife, a Type S personality. A little understanding goes a long way. In the event that you didn't spend much time on the DiSC personalities portion of this book, I highly recommend revisiting it.

You Want Me to Do What?

Expectations not being met lead to disappointment. But ask yourself, have you clearly defined and stated your expectations of each other? Without defining what you expect from someone you are not really giving them a fair chance to hit the target. It is also important to have reasonable expectations and respect that it's a reciprocal process. We learned earlier that goals and achievements are best accomplished when clearly defined and broken into smaller, achievable tasks. If you feel like the expectations you have for your partner aren't being met then first examine them. Are the expectations being communicated to them clearly? Are they reasonable or reduced into requests that are likely to feel achievable by your partner? If not, try taking this approach before allowing yourself to feel disappointment. You might find that this is an easy fix and a great way to accomplish some goals that you have together.

I Don't Have Time to Do Everything I Need to Do!

If you feel like you just don't have enough time to do everything that you need to do within the context of your marriage, please answer the following questions:

Do you have a plan as a couple?

Do you regularly offer to help the other?

Is your routing efficient? Meaning is one of you passing by places regularly that the other goes out of their way to reach? Is everything in your "routine" necessary?

These are basic questions regarding planning and efficiency. Having some kind of plan and open communication is the best place to start. That alone might give you back several hours a week. Then by putting some thought into ways you can create additional efficiency or perhaps even remove stuff from your routine, you can gain back needed time. Think of the "jar of change" example I gave early in the book. It might not seem like much when you save two minutes, one minute, five minutes, and so on, but over the course of longer periods of time these small sums can pile up into a significant amount of time. Remember, small changes can create big results.

DO THESE KIDS COME WITH AN OWNER'S MANUAL?

While often the biggest source of pride, joy, and love in our lives, our kids can also be the greatest source of stress. Unfortunately there is no playbook, definitive owner's manual, or toll-free support line when it comes to your kids. Sometimes this stress is due to situations we might be able to control, other times not.

As parents all of us are in different situations. Some families have both parents present, some don't. Some parents work full-time, some don't. Whichever situation applies to you one thing that is guaranteed is that you will have an overwhelming amount of information to process and decisions to make. And as the parenthood timeline changes, so will the context of these choices.

Knowing that all of our situations and personal beliefs are going to be unique, I'm not here to tell you HOW to be a parent. You are on your own on that one. Instead I want to address some ways that you can balance being an available and positive parent with the other parts of your life.

No One Gets a Twenty-Six-Hour Day

When your children are young you will be tasked with learning an entirely new process. The way you manage your time can have a big impact on your happiness. You are likely to feel exhaustion on unfamiliar levels. This is where trying to find balance is more important than ever. You aren't going to be great at everything right away but you will get it figured out. Try to find efficiencies wherever possible. Remember rest is critical. You aren't going to make quality decisions or produce quality results when in a sleepless state.

The demanding and sporadic schedule that comes with parenting makes personal efficiency more important than ever. Rather than saying, "I don't have enough time," make more! Start by examining everything you do and answering these questions:

Are you able to stop and accomplish different errands while out doing other ones?

Would getting anything ready the night before prevent feeling rushed in the morning?
Are there tasks you can complete while in other tasks' "down time"?

IMPORTANCE OF MAKING YOURSELF HAPPY TOO

While this might at first sound selfish it is crucial. In regard to parenting this statement always makes me think about a mom with five kids. She is always driving to sports practices, piano lessons, school pickup then drop-off only to come home to even more to do. She never gets to do anything for herself. It is okay to feel great about being this person. In fact on many levels you are my hero because I'm pretty sure I couldn't pull it off. The problem is that eventually you are going to find yourself far from balanced.

If we can't find happiness ourselves then it is really hard to support others seeking it. Yes, helping everyone else be awesome can and will make you happy. The only thing I am saying is that you need to find precious moments when you can do something for *you* to relax and recharge. If you are in a relationship with someone who seems like the person I just described, find a way to help this happen. Balance is a package deal.

WHY WON'T YOU LIVE LIFE THE WAY I WANT YOU TO?!

Sometimes we want more for our children than they want for themselves. This can result in frustration, disappointment, and negativity for parents. Add in children's need for independence and freedom as they get older and you'll begin to feel even more stressed and helpless. Instead of giving up or a strict lockdown, consider that watching them make their own choices is probably the best and least frustrating approach.

I am in no way saying that you should quietly stand there while your children play with fire. What I *am* saying is that no matter how much you want your children to do something, they aren't likely to do it, or at least with any spirit or success unless they want to. Expect to deal with some disappointment. That's just the way it goes sometimes. Allowing your kids to make their own decisions and then learn from the outcome ultimately helps produce more mature, independent, and intelligent future adults. That being said, I want to emphasize the "learn from the outcome" part of that statement. Letting your children make their own decisions, then immediately rushing in to fix the problem situations will only produce undesirable outcomes in the long run.

WHO ARE THESE PEOPLE RAISING MY CHILDREN?

In our modern world your children are going to absorb A LOT of information from A LOT of different sources. Dealing with input you can't always control such as their friends, media, teachers, and extended family members can be really stressful. You might at times feel like someone else is raising your kids for you. Finding the right people to take care of your children is important. Please consider this when comparing day care options or the different interactive situations your kids encounter. Negativity is lasting and contagious. While you might think children don't notice, they do! Remember or care about what is being done or said around them.

Acting in the same way that you would like your children to act is a good approach. Say to them the things you would feel comfortable hearing yourself. This also goes for the situations you bring them into. While we are trying to make the best of it, the fact is not everyone else is seeking a positive and productive path. So try and keep that in mind with everything from what you are watching on television to those you let around your kids.

A FOOL FOR LOVE

The last major component of personal relationships is our romantic relationships. For some this can be the most powerful of all. I have seen people throw away just about everything they have or have worked toward as a result of breakdowns in their love life. Like any other relationship influencers, the wrong romantic partner can bring you down and create a major drag on your sense of happiness. That being said, I'm not going to attempt to give you a lot of romantic relationship advice. I'll leave that to trained professionals. Just do me a favor and next time it doesn't work out with the man or woman of your dreams, don't throw everything away. It's just not worth it. You are an amazing, capable, and positive person! If you look for others like you then eventually you will find happiness.

SECTION FOUR:

OTHER IMPORTANT RELATIONSHIPS

(FRIENDS,COWORKERS, AND YES, OURSELVES)

D O THE PEOPLE you associate with add value to your life? I don't mean in a monetary sense; I mean in a general sense. Are the nonfamilial relationships you have getting you in trouble or getting you closer to being a winner? You owe it to yourself to answer this question with brutal honesty. Why? Because in contrast to relationships with family, we can almost always control relationships with friends because you don't necessarily have to continue to associate with these people if they're bringing negativity into your life.

When I say we all have—or had—"that friend" or rather "frenemy" at one point or currently in our lives a name probably comes to mind. Understanding the cause and effect relationship that comes with the people we choose to spend time with is remarkably important. Why? Well it's because your success and failure in life can have a direct correlation to those you choose to associate with. This isn't just my opinion; it is a pretty well-known fact. Your peers when positive and productive can provide you with motivation, support, empowerment, and sometimes a healthy sense of competition or drive to be the best you possible.

Here are some characteristics that great friends exhibit:

- Trustworthy and honest
- Loyal and dependable
- Aren't judgmental about situations or people

- Supportive in positive or negative situations
- Have lighthearted attitudes and find the best in situations and people
- Good listeners and show empathy

Negative or toxic people do the exact opposite. They operate with a sense of jealousy toward your success or desire to succeed. Toxic people are likely to exhibit many of the following traits:

- A negative attitude or "vibe" about stuff
- Untrustworthy
- Display bullying tendencies
- Regularly exhibit selfish behavior
- Seem to constantly have drama in their life
- Can act resentful when others seem happy
- Tend to gossip a lot
- Are freeloaders or someone you might refer to as a "mooch"

If you recognize people like this around you and you have control of your environment, you might want to consider replacing the time you spend with them with a higher-value activity.

DRINKING, GOSSIP, AND ALL THINGS NEGATIVITY

We could probably have a lengthy debate over what level of value certain parts of our social lives produce. Any action we choose has some kind of value based on its ability to either create balance in your life or move you closer to achieving one of your goals.

If your personal life seems out of balance, it could be that you are spending far too much time out drinking or on other social activities with minimal value. Maybe you're partaking in a lot of gossiping. Let's just be realistic—when you're gossiping with people you're usually not saying, "Oh my gosh! Did you see what she did last week? It was absolutely wonderful and amazing!" Face it, people who gossip are usually insecure and only feel better through judging others usually in a hurtful way. Keep in mind that participating in gossip isn't just saying it. Listening counts too.

On the flip side in certain situations getting some social activity might be what you *need* to get your mind off other things that could be occurring in your professional and physical life. I'm not saying that all social activity is bad, but for many people who feel out of balance the social aspect of their personal life is the culprit.

Let's go back to drinking or going out or whatever you're doing that is maybe a little excessive. The effects of those decisions can indirectly impact time slots in your life far past the actual time that you're doing the action.

For example, Friday night you go out with your friends. You meet them at 8:00 p.m. and have quite a few cocktails until 1:00 a.m., at which point you're a little hazy and don't exactly remember the last hour that you were out. You go home and pass out on the couch.

You normally wake up at 8:00 a.m. the next day and usually don't feel like someone just punched you in the face fifty times. Had you not gone overboard drinking, you might have woken up the next morning feeling healthy, strong, and motivated, with the ability to accomplish something positive in your life. Instead what you're finding is a hangover that keeps you miserable in bed until noon and you end up wiping the whole day's worth of opportunities off your calendar. That is now the price of the social decision you made the night before.

So going forward I want you to hold yourself accountable for your social decisions. It's very important if you want to try to make some improvements. I am not saying that you should avoid going out with friends. But if you are trying to do a better job of evaluating and analyzing the decisions you make coupled with the impact that they bring, then you will need to take ownership of your decisions when determining how badly you really want to achieve your goals in life.

Friendly Influence?

The friends we choose are a pretty important part of our program because the people in your personal and professional life have a pivotal effect on the outcome of your life whether you realize that or not. And a lot of that has to do with the input and energy they give you. If I give you five seconds to consider who your most valuable and positive friends are and then think about the opposite, I bet that all of you probably have a name, if not multiple names, that pop up under each category.

So that being said, if you hang out with a bunch of people who are up to no good and don't have much of a plan in life, you'll probably end up in that same category. And a lot of it has to do with the fact that we are most likely to perform within the same capacity of those around us. If you hang out with people who value accomplishment and leadership, and are getting positive things done in their lives, you're going to feel a need or desire to do the same with yours. But if you're constantly around people who don't value positive and productive outcomes, then you most likely won't either.

NEGATIVITY IS CONTAGIOUS

When we think about contagious things, what first comes to mind is catching a cold or the flu. But there are other things that can be contagious, such as moods, thoughts, and attitudes. If you're around someone who is in a good mood, after a while you'll find yourself in a good mood too. Similarly, being around someone who drains your energy and gives you all the reasons something won't work will ultimately drag you down as you adopt their thoughts. Would you be excited about going into a room where you knew everyone had a cold? So why knowingly put yourself in situations where you can catch a bad case of negativity?

PROFESSIONAL RELATIONSHIPS

Interactions at work (or with those you do business with) can be just as powerful as interactions with family and friends. Why? Well there are a number of reasons. Your professional efforts probably provide—or at least help provide—for the welfare of your family. Any feeling of success or things that might limit you can in turn create more emotional feelings. You also probably spend a fair amount of time at work and often in an environment that offers less control than what you have in your personal life. The last influencing factor is that people often correlate their professional success with their identity and overall success in life. So the relationships, experiences, and results associated with your professional life can easily influence your personal and then your physical life.

Let's look at a situation that all of us are likely to have experienced, which is a strained or tense relationship with a boss or coworker. When this is present in your life and especially when these situations are at their more uncomfortable moments, do you just leave it at the door at 5:00 p.m. when you depart for the day? Probably not. It is more likely that you carry it with you into your personal time away from work. More specifically you find these situations dominating your thought process or conversations with friends and family.

So what's the solution for improving relationships in your personal and professional life? It starts with

112

having some understanding. By that I mean understanding the situation, the people involved, and yourself too. Using the information you found in the DiSC section of this book you can gain a better understanding of how your personality blends or interacts with those you work with as well as those around you in your personal life. The results can be astonishing. It is important to remember that the moments in your life involving others are exchanges, meaning there is a give and take aspect. Regardless of how unreasonable you might believe someone else or a situation to be, there is another side too. The great part about that is your input into these exchanges is something that you *can* in fact control and be aware of. The same goes for your reactions. Having a strong understanding of your personality type and how it interacts with others, more specifically what other people are likely to respond favorably to, will do nothing other than benefit you. Also have an open mind. It could be YOU who is causing or inflaming the situation.

If you have a negative relationship in your professional life that never seems to go away, try addressing it. Leaving negative situations alone often just makes them worse. Be a calm and reasonable adult and try to "talk it out." More often than not you are going to find a positive result from this approach. Now be prepared for a little discomfort on the way to positivity. But once communication starts to open up, all parties will have a foundation for creating communication.

Whether you are the owner of the company or an intern arriving for your first day at work, the following tips and suggestions can help improve not only your situation in the workplace but also the people around you.

- Recognize others' hard work and achievements
- Be proactive in your approach to dealing with potential problems
- Avoid showing favoritism
- Don't drag your personal life and problems to work with you
- Show up on time for work and meetings
- Be a good listener when others are presenting solutions and proposals
- Define goals and expectations
- Be positive in your approach to problem-solving
- Try to always present a solution when bringing up a problem

Be Nice to Yourself

We've talked about relationships with people around you. Now let's talk about the relationship we have with ourselves. I like to say be nice to yourself. This is a pretty big deal if you're not. Our self-confidence or lack thereof is created by our own internal conversations.

And when I say internal conversations you're not crazy for having them. We all constantly tell ourselves we *can* or we *can't*. Being nice to yourself means not bombarding your thoughts with reasons why you can't, or reasons why you aren't perfect. Instead try replacing that cruel voice with one that speaks louder than the one criticizing you. Demand that your positive and productive thoughts have a louder voice than the negative ones.

All of this stuff is going on in your head all day every day. Being aware and attempting to improve it can have a remarkable effect on you. As you continue to have thoughts of what you can and cannot do, get in the habit of asking yourself: *Am I being nice to myself?* How would you feel if someone outside your head expressed the same doubts and fears? Would that be someone you wanted to be around or someone you'd get away from as fast as you could?

Things we do all day to create self-pity can easily be changed but it does require realignment of our thought process. Once again use replacement to literally swap negative mental chatter for more positive remarks. Start seeing negative things that we tell ourselves as the problem and replace the problem thought with solution-based thinking.

The bottom line is that improving the quality of ALL of your relationships is invaluable. Accept that you too need to be on a mission of continued improvement when it comes to relationships and the positive results will follow.

A Conversation with
Fashion Expert Vincent Boucher

Vincent Boucher is a writer, fashion journalist, and stylist to the stars. As a fashion editor he has worked for major magazines such as *Esquire* and *New York*. He has also been a longtime celebrity stylist in Hollywood, working with clients such as Kiefer Sutherland, Teri Hatcher, Jessica Alba, and Josh Groban to name a few.

MATT: Being in the fashion industry must be tough. By that I mean the highly subjective nature of the decisions and choices you made probably meant a lot of opinions were generated after. How did you handle that and did it ever seem to cause an imbalanced feeling in your life?

VINCENT: You're talking about image making, which is intensely personal. Multiply that by the publicity factor of a Hollywood celebrity and there are a number of opinions that enter in—yours and your subjects' opinion, the public's opinion, and the studio's opinion. In some ways you're always trying to make your case and recommend because you're the authority. You have to come to it with positivity. Sometimes there were other opinions that were intensely frustrating. I've been doing this a long time so you have to separate your recommendations or ideas for this person, and even though that's an extension of yourself, it's not you. They're not criticizing you. It's work. You have to think about it in a different space. It's almost like a character. It didn't happen instantly; it took a long time to learn.

Because it is about a person and what they're going to wear themselves, whether they're going to be photographed or on the red carpet, your job is to make them happy. It's a personal failing if you don't come to the party with lots of different ideas. You may have your heart set on one particular look, but when that doesn't work out, you have to go to plan B and be happy about it. But it's always going to work out.

When I worked at *Esquire* I had a motto to myself that the magazine is never going to print a blank page. There's going to be something on that page. If it doesn't work in the moment, if people are disagreeing, or it's not going well, in the end there's not going to be a blank page in the magazine. If something isn't going to work out one way, it's not the end of the world. That's experience talking—if you can see that, that's helpful.

In terms of disappointment—of course! If you've worked really hard on something, and it gets set aside or someone doesn't like it, it's disappointing. What I've found over long experience is it doesn't help to make the person who disagrees with you the object of your "ire" even though that's the first thing people tend to do. It's business. It's hard to do, but on some level, you just have to say, "It's business, and I might be working with that person again, whether it's tomorrow or three years down the road." You have to think this way, especially if you're a freelance or entrepreneurial entity. You don't have the luxury of popping off to someone you disagree with. You can, but it usually doesn't work out very well. You have to find other ways to deal with it. Talking to friends can be helpful but, especially in Hollywood, I didn't want to go into a lot of the personal business when it was personal—it gets gossipy. Then it makes it more part of my life, harder to separate. You have to find other ways to think about it. For me, I'd plan another personal experience that took me out of that head, or I'd go work out. Reading really transports me. When I was in LA, I would go for a drive and let it all kind of wash out.

What you said about it being business and the recognition of having to continue to work with people: how did you deal with the difficult people in your world? Was there a particular technique or something you did to deal with it when it was right in your face?

If you can, just keep your cool. Even if you're met with disappointment, if you can keep positive and cool and not get ruffled, that relieves tension. People who are high-strung or enablers do it sometimes just because they can, or they want to get a rise out of you. I'm not just saying only in Hollywood, it's all over. Don't engage, because they just want to get some sort of response. If you keep yourself on a professional level, it short circuits temperaments.

Along the way to any successful destination, there's a lot of doubt. I've done things that went well, some not. I'm assuming there's a fair amount of turnover in Hollywood. How did you get through feelings of doubt, hesitation, or lack of confidence?

I was put into a big role early in my career. I worked at *Esquire*. It was a general interest magazine for men that also happened to have a fashion section. The people I reported to weren't fashion people. So I had to explain to them what my concept was—why it was important and why it would work, which was a much different thing than working at a fashion magazine where it's already part of the fashion world and you're talking about the trends or fashion designers. I had many years in the general interest field where I had to explain myself and make my case. When I went freelance and later went to Hollywood that was a skillset that helped. When you're trying to convince a nervous actress that something is right for her and it's something she hadn't thought of, you have to be able to make your case. And you have to deal with the times they won't agree with you. And that's fine, too. When you're working as a freelancer, obviously you want the best result for your own "glory," but you're really in a service industry and unless everyone goes away happy, you haven't done your job.

Did you travel a lot?

I traveled some in LA. I went to New York and Europe with clients. When I was styling in New York, I worked as a stylist for both editorial magazines and fashion companies like Tommy Hilfiger and Nautica. And we would do big fashion shoots and fashion shows on the road, so I traveled quite a bit then.

Did the travel present problems with your personal, professional, and physical parts of your life?

There was a period in the late-nineties in New York when I was working for a lot of different companies and it seemed like I was out of town every other month. I remember feeling that time was really going by. Hours I was working were long but it was a dilemma because the money was really good. I'd get home and think, "Gee, what happened the last three months?" I was out of touch with my friends. When I moved to LA, it was something I really liked for a long time—I was there most of the time.

Were there flags that signaled imbalance in your life? Any indicators for you?

I wasn't taking the best care of myself—eating whatever was around. Fashion is very work intensive to begin with. It takes hours to make things happen and then put travel hours on top of that. I never experienced physical problems, but I would miss whatever regime I was on that was interrupted. I would lose my sense of place—sometimes wondering where I belonged. Because I was always traveling to different places sometimes there were opportunities to see or do something. I would try to squeeze in those opportunities. But sometimes I would come home after a big trip and feel kind of empty.

What would be your recommendations to get a sense of balance in one's life?

The biggest thing, and it's hard for people to do, is don't overpromise. So many people will say "yes" because they feel they should, but later they wonder why they did. None of us is perfect and we've all had moments when we said yes to something and wish we wouldn't have. But outside of the normal kinds of obligations I think that's a big key thing for me. Always decide what you want to do. Saying yes just to be saying yes doesn't benefit you in the end. If it's not something you really want, need, or have to do, then you're probably going to resent it. I think that kind of thing is even more harmful than a lot of travel. It brings negativity because you've been forced into a situation. You have to remember not to overpromise when you have a choice. And you DO have a choice. I'm also talking about things in your personal and physical life, not just work.

122

Do you currently or have you ever had written goals? Did you find that to be helpful?

I have at various times in my life. I think any time you make a commitment, it's much more concrete than if you're just thinking about it. I don't have a specific example, but because I'm in a deadline business, I am used to writing down when deadlines and certain things have to occur, so in a way that's a similar process. So you write it down, you have to accomplish it by X date.

SECTION FIVE:

CREATING FINANCIAL BALANCE

THE BEST DEFINITION I can give of *financial success* is "when you are no longer worried about money." Yes it's a very broad answer but it's going to be different for everybody depending on who you are, the surrounding conditions, and even your personality style. For instance, one person might feel financially relieved to have $10,000 in the bank, while the same balance might give another cause for panic. Perspective is always personal.

Want Versus Need

With money, one thing that everyone can agree, impulsive decisions can get you in serious trouble. From this point forward let's start training ourselves to clearly define whether something we're going to purchase is a *need* or a *want*. There is a very definitive line between the two.

Things in life that are truly needs are a fairly short list: shelter, food, water, air, and health care. Almost everything else outside of that is a want: a nicer car, new clothes, exotic vacation, second home, etc. Now if you don't have any decent clothes and they're required for your job, that's a need and we can accept that. Buying a new dress to wear for the party on Friday is a want, especially if you already have a whole bunch of them hanging in the closet. Purchasing a new watch or iPhone because the latest and greatest model just came out or online shopping for shoes that style magazines declare the hottest Hollywood trend are also examples of getting things that you want, not need.

Our personalities, especially the D and I types, can lead us to be impulsive. We see things and we have to have them. To help, there are some self-control strategies that can separate needs from wants when it comes to financial control. One of them is never buying anything the first time you see it. Force yourself to think about it. If you go into a store and see something you really want or think you need, give yourself a day or two and see if you still feel that way. The fact of the matter is if you have financial problems, you need to earn more, spend less, or do both. Removing impulsivity from your spending is extremely important and instantly beneficial.

MANAGING INCOME

The goal is to get you in the position where monthly bills, debt, and your overall finances are not keeping you in a state of dread or panic. There are a lot of factors that can lead to poor financial health. Let's begin with income. Perhaps you used to have more of it than you do now. Or maybe you make good money yet never seem to have enough to cover expenses. Financial worry is often related to our own inability to manage personal finances and funds. Parkinson's Law is a financial rule that states that expenses will rise to meet income. Basically what that means is you are going to spend everything you make. If you make more money you're probably going to spend more money.

Take a look at these eye-opening statistics:

In a survey[3] of more than twenty-five thousand people, 36 percent spent about equal to their income and 19 percent spent more than their income. Over half didn't have three months' worth of expenses saved up in case of emergency, and over a third made only minimum credit card payments.

It's no surprise that money is often the root of stress and related imbalance in our lives.

TYPES OF DEBT

Certain debts are typically part of life: home and vehicle. A third debt that is becoming more and more prominent, especially with young people, is educational debt. These three types of debt can be sizeable and ongoing for very long periods of time. A standard home loan is anywhere between fifteen to thirty years. And by the time you reach your last car payment it's likely time for a *new* car . . . and you start payments all over again. Student debt can follow you for years after graduation. How then do we go about handling debt and what are some of the best ways we can teach ourselves to be more financially responsible?

---

[3] Ballenger, Brandon. "Study: 19 Percent of Americans Spend More Than They Earn." *Money Talks News.* Money Talks News, 10 June 2013. Web. 07 Nov. 2016.

Recurring Debt and the Factor of Twelve

When it comes to budgeting, I like to use what I call the Factor of Twelve. This is applied to all things that have recurring monthly payments or subscriptions. What used to be 100 percent purchased products have now turned into subscriptions, such as magazines, digital music services, and bundled packages of cable television, digital phone, and cellular plans. This is a model that a lot of businesses now prefer in order to generate recurring revenue. And since the monthly amounts seem *individually* manageable it's easy to lose sight of the *cumulative* annual cost we absorb.

Applying the Factor of Twelve forces you to consider the "hidden" annual cost. So a $25-a-month subscription is actually $300 a year ($25/month x twelve months). Given this formula, I want you to review your bank and credit card statements and compile all the things that you routinely buy or participate in that generate a monthly bill. Now multiply each monthly cost by twelve and then add them all together. You're probably going to be very surprised at the resulting number you spend on such things each year.

For example, let's take the subscription for the extra tier of cable television that you're using to take up large blocks of low value. We'll guess it costs a $100 a month. I'm not saying that you shouldn't have cable television, but you don't truly need hundreds of pay channels that add up to an extra $1200 a year. If you're looking for "extra" funds to help pay off high interest-accruing credit card balances, they're probably right in front of you. This exercise takes a little planning and minor readjustment but is well worth it in the long run.

Credit Card Debt

To get an even stronger grip on alleviating financial pressures we need to discuss universally dreaded credit card debt. For *any* kind of debt financial institutions charge a certain percentage of interest. Credit cards are almost undoubtedly going to be significantly higher in imposed interest rates than house, car, education, and home improvement loans. And the highest interest rates generally stem from cards or "special financing" associated with retail, including department, furniture, and "big box" stores. These may woo you in with a one-time discount but then you likely overspend and are burdened with high interest rate debt that soon outweighs any initial deal. Another common scenario is a promotional interest rate, such as zero percent interest for X number of months. This is acceptable only if you have the ability to pay the full amount within the number of months in the promotional period.

Keep in mind what the stores hope for is that you DON'T pay the account off within the promotional period. Not doing so will almost always backdate an absurd interest rate to the original purchase date and then saddle you with a high interest debt until paid off. This is the equivalent of a wolf in sheep's clothing. While it seems gentle at first it may very well bite you right in the wallet.

Another thing to consider if you go into a situation that is offering zero percent financing is that the store actually takes a hefty charge to offer the attractive deal. Depending on the length of the contract they may be paying anything from 5 to 12 percent of your total purchase to the bank in order to make that special financing possible. Turning this to your advantage, don't be afraid to ask for a discount if you're not using their promotional rate.

It's essential that we understand our "big picture" financial condition. Start by making a list of *all* your monthly payments and in the column next to them, include what percentage of interest you are paying. To give you an idea of how this works, let's say you have $5,000 in credit card debt that is being charged 18 percent interest. You also have a $15,000 car loan that is charging 6 percent interest. Your $5,000 debt on your credit card will be charging as much interest as your car payment, which is three times higher than that amount. One of the things that we are trying to do is chip away the debt that you are carrying on the highest interest rate. Eliminating those first frees up extra money for you to attack your other debt.

You might have $15,000 cash sitting in a checking or savings account. You might also have a credit card with a $10,000 balance accruing interest at a high rate. It is possible that having the cash in your bank account gives you a feeling of security. However, this feeling of security is pretty expensive. Hoarding cash in the bank which is earning less than 1 percent interest versus using it to pay toward debt that's charging you anywhere from 12 to 25 percent interest is a financially bad idea. But the mistake is a lot more common than you might think. You're most likely saving that cash in your bank account in case of an emergency. While I'm all for having money in case of an emergency, you can use that credit card in the event of an emergency. But a rising mountain of debt is just another form of emergency. For anyone in that scenario, I suggest that you consider paying off your credit card in full rather than hoarding cash.

TRACKING EXPENSES

If you aren't currently tracking your monthly expenses and want to have an eye-opening experience, do it! There are a lot of software, free online programs, and apps available for personal financial planning that allow you to track your expenses. If you do that diligently for a couple of months you'll be able to see exactly where your money goes. I guarantee there will be some surprises. You'll most likely find spending that you didn't realize was so high for certain things. You will also most likely realize how much money you spend on trivial things that are certainly considered "wants" rather than "needs." Using the concept of replacement now try to replace some unneeded purchasing with payment toward your debts. If that feels difficult take a minute and hold yourself accountable for the debt you created for yourself. The same kind of spending that you are about to eliminate is what created this situation after all.

Pay Yourself First

Paying yourself first has several meanings. In a financial sense, contributing to some sort of savings plan before you start spending your paycheck builds financial security and outsmarts Parkinson's Law. It means saving before you do anything else. It doesn't have to be a tremendous amount, but a little each paycheck will yield big results over time.

The best and easiest way to pay yourself is to do it automatically. Meaning don't even give yourself the chance to spend the money.

Home Loans and Mortgages

When purchasing a home, consider the total length of the loan. For example, not everyone can purchase a house on a lower total interest fifteen-year loan as opposed to a standard loan for thirty years. To show you the difference, if you look at an amortization table on your thirty-year home loan, you would probably want to cry. The longer the loan is, the less of the principal you're paying off each month. Many people who have purchased their first home find themselves shocked when they start getting their statements. For instance, a hypothetical $200,000 home obtained with a thirty-year loan may entail a $1,500-a-month house mortgage payment. But—especially in the loan's early years—of the $1,500 a mere $137 went toward the principal of the loan.

If you purchase the same home on a fifteen-year loan, the payment is higher each month but you would actually, from your first payment forward, pay off substantially more principal than interest. If you were to purchase a thirty-year loan, you hit that same point fifteen years into it. This is some of the decision-making you'll need to weigh, especially if you make big, long-term commitments. It can make a huge difference. Knowing your fixed costs allows for easier planning and understanding of your upcoming expenses.

Something as little as a quarter of a percent on a thirty-year home loan can equate to tens of thousands of dollars. This is a situation where technology is your friend and can help you get a grip on personal spending and expenses. Remember, a lot of this is about awareness. Any time you're about to incur debt and it comes with payments, keep in mind that it's going to continue on and on until the end of the payments. If at the beginning of the loan you're already concerned about your ability to pay in a timely manner, it's probably putting a little too much pressure on you.

Some people don't know that the interest you're paying on your home loan is tax deductible. Let's say you purchase a home with a monthly payment of $1000. When you purchase your home, your monthly payment is referred to as PITI, an acronym that stands for principal, interest, taxes, and insurance. The *principal* is the amount of money that is left outstanding on the loan. *Interest* is the rate or percentage of the outstanding loan that you pay to the bank. *Taxes* are property taxes based on the locale of your home, which vary by city, state, or country. *Insurance* is an amount of the loan that covers your home in case of a catastrophic event.

On our example of a house payment of $1,000, the interest is $500 a month ($6,000 for the year). You're allowed a deduction on your tax return for that interest. That interest is actually transferred directly to your tax return so that $6,000 annual interest amount will then be allowed as $6,000 income on your tax return from which they won't pull any federal taxes. You still pay your local and state taxes on it but your federal income tax rate will not apply to that. Now we look at that $6,000 in income if you're at a 25 percent tax rate. That would be $1500 a year that you're going to save on taxes based on interest deduction. So if we look at that, the real money out-of-pocket that you're paying every month for your home isn't $1000 a month. It will be in the ballpark of $880 due to the future tax savings. The government wants to encourage you to buy your home so that's one way they currently give you added benefits.

Car Loans

Unless you're investing in rare and classic cars, most cars are horrible investments. It's not even really an investment. The term "investment" can apply to your house because even though real estate markets ebb and flow, historically over a long period of time your home will still end up being worth more than what you paid for it. The way I look at purchasing a car is that your thought process should be: "I am willing to not have X amount of money over the next five years in exchange for the privilege of driving this car." Let's say you buy a new car for $30,000. Five to six years later it's probably going to be worth 30 percent of what you paid.

The minute you drive your car off the lot, it loses about 10 percent of its value, and by the end of the first year, another 10 percent. A new car continues to lose value for four more years, so on the average, a new car loses 60 percent of its total value over the first five years.[4]

The good news is that car manufacturers are now making safer vehicles that last longer, so people are keeping their cars for longer periods of time.

---

[4] Davis, Martin. "Car Depreciation: 5 Things to Consider I CARFAX." Carfax.com. CARFAX, n.d. Web. 07 Nov. 2016.

Student Loans

The cost of higher education continues to rise and in turn more graduates are coming out of school with a sizeable debt load. At one point when I had student debt I was lucky enough that I didn't have an extreme amount. I think I had $30,000, which is still a lot but far from many of today's graduates' burden. What I discovered along the way is that my loan consisted of several smaller loans bundled into one. For example, you might have a $6,000 Stafford loan that actually comes as a $2,500 loan and a $3,500 loan. The interest rate may vary from one semester to the next due to the different interest rates of each "sub" loan. I figured this out because when I was at the point of repaying my student loan I looked at my credit report and realized that I had *seven* different loans that were all charging varied percentages of interest. So my monthly payment of somewhere in the ballpark of $300 was being equally divided across all seven loans.

Two of the seven loans had a 1.5 percent higher interest rate than the others. I was able to get into my account online and reconfigure my loan repayment plan so my entire monthly payment first went toward the loans that had the highest rates. By doing this it enabled me to pay off all of them faster. Also from a credit scenario, my credit score went up substantially because I was viewed as successfully paying loans off in an acceptable amount of time.

Debt to Income Ratio (DTI)

While understanding debts and interest it is important to understand what is known as DTI—Debt to Income Ratio. This is the proportionate amount of recurring monthly payments compared to your overall income.

DTI is based on a monthly calculation. The way it works is the bank looks at the minimum credit card payment, your house payment (that includes the principal, interest, taxes, and insurance), car payments, student loan debts, and any other recurring debt. This is specifically debt-related, so it won't include things like monthly subscriptions, utility bills, or gym memberships, etc.

So if you have a $2,000 monthly commitment to pay off debt and a $6,000 income (they look at your income before tax) then you would have a 33 percent DTI. Most lenders consider a 36 percent DTI to be the limit before you become risky for them. There are different scenarios and calculations that places like banks, auto loan entities, and other lenders use.

$$\frac{\text{Sum of Debt Payments}}{\text{Income (Pre Tax)}} = \text{Debt to Income Ratio}$$

DEBT TO INCOME RATIO	LENDERS SEE YOUR DEBT LEVEL AS
< 15%	Very Good
16% - 20%	Good
21% - 35%	Try to Reduce Debt
36% - 50%	Too Much Debt
> 50%	Serious Trouble

Why is your DTI so relevant? If one of your goals is to own your own home, it's critical to see how recurring debt could effect your ability to purchase a home. If your DTI is high, then the mortgage lender will charge you a higher percentage rate—if you even qualify. If it's low they are far more likely to give you a loan and charge you a lower rate. Having some understanding of where you fall in a DTI calculation is important because once you get on the wrong side of it, it becomes very difficult to do *a lot* of stuff. Banks are pretty good at determining what you may or may not have the ability to repay. This information is freely passed back and forth among the credit-rating agencies and financial institutions. If the bank is telling you that your DTI is high then that should be a major red flag waving in front of you. Continuing to find little pieces of your total monthly debt to chop and take out of the equation is the best bet to get DTI playing in your favor.

Ask for a Discount!

Asking for a discount is a potential windfall that not enough people do. Any time you're shopping ask for a discount. It's pretty simple. Now this isn't going to necessarily work or be the greatest tool at Walmart, the grocery store checkout line, or other places that clearly have set pricing on their merchandise. But there are a number of products such as jewelry, furniture, home appliances, electronics, and vehicles that when talking to the salesperson or company representative you can use one simple phrase: *Is this the best price you can give me?*

If you can get in the habit of asking that pretty much wherever you go there are a lot of places where you can really get a lot better deals than the prices on their price tags. They have that price and have it high because they're hoping that you don't use the phrase: Is this the best price you can give me? I assure you that if you go out and try it you will run into a situation where you might save yourself hundreds if not thousands of dollars. It's kind of a weird feeling too because in the back of your head you realize, *Oh. . . so you would let me go ahead and pay this really high price had I not said anything.* The thing is a lot of people honestly are too scared or timid to ask. But you've got nothing to lose. Remember you're in a business doing business and it's good business for you personally to try to get the best price and keep the most money in your pocket as possible. You don't have to be a pain in the butt and you should never be rude about it. Actually you'll find you're going to draw a whole lot more flies with honey, so don't be afraid to use the phrase: Is this the best price you can give me?

TAX REFUNDS

Most people look at their tax return and view it favorably—or not based on whether they got a refund. That can be a really shortsighted way to look at things. If you were to get a $1500 refund at the time you filed your taxes, what that really means is that you loaned the government $1500 and they're now giving it back to you. It's always been your money.

There are various calculation tools that can help you gain a better understanding. Basically you shouldn't be looking at the possibility of a tax refund as an annual payday. You could actually with a little bit of planning have that money in your pocket all along. There are also a tremendous amount of tax credits or breaks out there for all kinds of individuals. I'm not going to go into a whole lot of them, but there are several situations based on if you're a Native American or an ex-member of the military. If you're a business owner there are tons of things, such as using certain types of cars that are fuel efficient or electric cars and stuff like that. With a little bit of research and planning you can possibly find a lot of money that you might otherwise leave on the table.

One of the biggest ways to improve both finances and overall imbalance is to succeed in our professional life. In the next section we will learn how to be more productive and happier in the work arena that plays a huge part of our identity and often feels like our "second home."

SECTION SIX:

KEEPING IT PROFESSIONAL

IT IS MY BELIEF that your perceived level of achievement at work has everything to do with whether or not you are happy with your job. Therefore, your ability to get where you want to be professionally has a big part in your ability to achieve balance in your life. In fact achieving a feeling of balance without some sense of professional fulfillment is going to be nearly impossible. This next section is dedicated to helping you understand in practical terms what it might take to get where you want to be in the workplace.

Work and career is a topic loved by some, hated by others. In fact when surveyed most Americans openly admit to not liking their job. The reality for most of us is that we have to work in order to support ourselves and our family. So what's the problem? It's not that people in general don't like working. I actually believe most people do in fact like being productive. The issue is that many people aren't doing everything they are capable of, feel stuck or underappreciated, and maybe just don't work well with others.

This section of *Balance Me* will help you find more success not only at your job but through revealing what your employer, employees, or coworkers want and expect from you too. Being able to achieve everything you want from a job isn't just about you. It includes the people you work with and your ability to have healthy and productive relationships with them. By helping them find their own success you're better equipped for your own.

Learning how to have the most beneficial and efficient experience at the workplace can make achieving balance in your life far easier. So whether you're a business owner, manager, or in a sales or a service position, I'm going to point out some of the most common areas where inefficiencies occur and give you some solutions for improvement. My goal is to create efficiencies within your business that lower the stress in your life. Less stress will lead to a more enjoyable, productive, and healthy personal and physical life. And far better balance.

Working with Others

Earlier we saw how our personality style interacts with others. It's important to remember that work relationships are a two-way street. It doesn't matter if you are the owner of the company, the manager, someone with an entry-level position, or a part-time intern hoping to get a job, *all* relationships involve more than just you. We are most likely going to get what we want by helping others do the same. What does that have to do with relationships? Everything. When the people you work with understand that you are on their side and have a general interest in their success you now have the foundation needed to build a successful and productive relationship. This doesn't mean that you are going to spend day after day without differences. But you will have what is needed to build mutual respect that allows an understanding of each other's role in your workplace.

That sounds too easy, right? Well in some ways it might be. Where things begin to go astray is when people want different things. Or maybe the exact same thing and there's no room to share. But overall it should be your priority to treat others with dignity and respect and try to be a productive member of the team.

Why is all of this important when it comes to feeling a sense of balance in your life? If you are in a stressful, unproductive, negative, or combative environment day in and day out then it is going to be hard to just leave that at the office door when you return home each day. It is also going to create a sense of anxiety when it comes to going back to that environment each morning. If we can find ways to be at peace or more successful when it comes to our professional life, we are going to have a much easier time outside of it.

WORKPLACE AWARENESS

Are you aware of how the things you say or do at work are viewed by others? You should be, as in many ways it is the controlling factor when it comes to your future in that enterprise. Or if you own the business it shapes how interested your employees are in helping the business succeed. The principle of "perception is reality" is especially true in the workplace. So let's go over a few things I believe will be remarkably helpful when it comes to you finding more success in your work.

BE DEPENDABLE

I placed this first because this is where it all starts. If you can't be dependable then you can't be successful professionally. Begin with getting to work on time. Period. If you are a "late" person, then figure out how to fix it. Leave fifteen minutes earlier, get up earlier—just figure out how to get to work on time. Nothing says "I don't care" more than the person who is habitually late to work. And everyone notices even if they aren't saying something. Being late to work, meetings, and other work-related functions is a career killer.

That being said, don't be the person who seems to need to leave work early day in and day out either, as that is more or less the same thing. I know, none of this sounds that fun, but I'm here to help you, not sugarcoat the reality of the workplace.

The final ingredient is to try and avoid being what I refer to as a "track star." You know, the person who sprints out the door the moment it is 5:00 p.m., or whatever time your shift ends. That doesn't mean you need to work late every single day or even regularly. Just try and have a sense of whether or not you are leaving other people in a spot where they are going to have to stay even later to finish collective tasks. One of the very best ways to show that you care—and to build lasting and meaningful relationships with your employer, employees, or coworkers—is to simply ask at the end of each day, "Is there anything you need help with before I leave?"

DELIVER ON YOUR PROMISES, OR DON'T MAKE THEM!

Keep your promises, or just don't make promises. It is pretty common to hear me say, "The only thing I'm willing to promise you is that things will change." If you choose to make promises then keeping them is a pretty big part of whether you are considered dependable or not. Avoid being someone who impulsively makes promises without consideration of what actions or resources will be needed to make them reality. Understand that what might be promised quickly or without consideration may actually be a pretty serious task for someone else. The word "promise" isn't taken lightly and neither is the lack of delivering of them.

Excuses. They are like . . . well, you know. While occasionally excuses are relevant, most of the time they are just us not being accountable for our own actions or lack thereof. A constant barrage of excuses will only make you seem unreliable and flaky. And even unbelievable when there's a *valid* reason why you didn't get the job done. What builds more respect and appreciation from others in the workplace is the ability to own up to any errors and shortfalls. Instead of making an excuse, try saying (and meaning) "I didn't get the job done the way I needed to; I understand that I need to do a better job next time." People don't expect you to be perfect. But they do expect you to be someone who tries to learn from errors in order to be better.

"Do or do not. There is no try." —Yoda

Keep It Professional

Are the things you say and do at work professional? Just because you show up and do your job doesn't mean you are being professional. After we work with others for a while we begin to feel more at ease around them. This makes it a lot easier to feel like we can open up to them. That isn't always a good move. First off, don't ever assume that someone shares your same opinions, especially when it comes to the topics of religion, politics, or sex. You literally have nothing to gain and everything to lose when you make comments about those subjects. Let me explain. When it comes to religion or politics the likelihood that others share your exact same view is minimal at best. So what do you have to gain by discussing either with a coworker? Absolutely nothing! Don't do it. When it comes to sex, that just shouldn't be something brought up in the workplace period.

LIMITING DISTRACTIONS

Part of keeping things professional is to limit the distractions that surround us. This starts with something most people have in their pocket or next to them all of the time—YOUR PHONE. I am positive that every one of you reading this just had a guilty culprit pop into their head. Hopefully that culprit isn't you. If it is, then you are not helping yourself when it comes to success at your job or with your coworkers. Once again, if you think everyone doesn't notice, THEY DO. Nothing annoys me more as an employer than seeing someone staring at their phone every time I see them.

Social media is another major source of distraction. How much work time is lost each day by people using social media? People in the United States check their Facebook, Twitter, and other social media accounts on average *seventeen* times a day, meaning at least every waking hour, if not more. The majority of compulsive social media checkers are adults, with the highest usage observed in those between the ages of 25–54. In the United States, people spend on average 4.7 hours per day on their phones. Considering that the average American is awake just over fifteen hours a day, we're spending approximately a third of our time on our phones—a significant chunk of the day.[5] Talk about a low-value activity. In my opinion, unless your job is in social media, you should be able to do social media in fifteen minutes a day. Most of what's on there is other people documenting their own low-value activities. Unplug from your phone and social media accounts and you can accomplish a few extra undistracted hours a day!

It's an epidemic in so many ways.

The final area of distraction I want to discuss is keeping your personal life, well, personal. I'm not saying that you shouldn't be friends on some level with your coworkers. In fact I believe it is healthy to do so. Just don't get into the habit of dumping all of your personal problems on them. Everyone has their own issues. You detailing all of yours day in and day out isn't going to help them or you. It can lead to the perception that your life is a mess and unless they are the person who is going to fix your problems then you probably aren't going to gain anything positive from sharing all of the details.

BE TRUSTWORTHY AND HONEST

Part of me feels like I should not even have to say this, but you'd be surprised. When people at work give you

---

[5] Chang, Lulu. "Americans Spend an Alarming Amount of Time Checking Social Media on Their Phones." *Digital Trends.* N.p., 13 June 2015. Web. 07 Nov. 2016.

information they trust that you aren't going to share it with everyone else. Others' ability to trust you is built over time but it can be destroyed in just moments. Don't ever fudge on a time card, misuse company expense accounts, or take credit for things you haven't done. It's pretty rare for untrustworthy people to find success in the workplace. The perception that you are untrustworthy is nearly impossible to shed and likely the path to no longer being employed.

DON'T BE OVERLY EMOTIONAL

No matter who you are or how successful you may be, it is certain that things won't always go your way. How well do you handle change and adversity? Your response to failure is critical. Many people are overly emotional in their immediate response to things failing. I even admit to this fault at times. Each personality type handles frustration and failure differently but we need to make sure to limit the emotional level of our responses. Our immediate response to these situations is a form of impulsivity. It is really easy to get caught up in the moment and say or do things that we normally wouldn't say or do. Therefore, it is important to be extra mindful of our reactions. If you are someone who is prone to emotional reactions, be aware of it and then do some simple forward-thinking about how you will react when you succeed or fail. This basic action will prepare your mind and hopefully your reaction to either result.

Don't Be Poor

<u>Poor communication</u> is the thing people complain most about within the workplace. It leads to a variety of problems that frustrate employees and business owners alike. Lack of communication will strain the productivity of any organization and is a major source of frustration. With all of the technology available to us, poor communication isn't something that should be occurring in any business. We have the ability to share each other's schedules, create to-do lists, and send e-mails from devices that are right at our fingertips.

<u>Poor planning</u>, or not planning at all, is another culprit when it comes to problems in the workplace. This is when employers and employees don't take the time to create well-thought-out plans for obtaining their goals. This lack of planning can lead to a whole string of wide-reaching problems.

<u>Poor execution</u> is the combined result of poor planning and communication. Follow-up is a key ingredient to produce better results. Are you creating measurable results? Are you creating reasonable time frames? Are you holding people accountable for their actions and results? These are all important things if you want to improve overall as a business or a professional.

<u>Poor delegation</u> – All you can do is all you can do! If you aren't delegating tasks effectively, then you are most likely facing serious inefficiency. Whether you are the owner of the business, the manager, or an entry-level contributor, you can only produce so much. Effective delegation isn't "being bossy;" it's actually great teamwork.

EAT YOUR FROG

If the first thing you had to do each day was eat a real live frog, would it help to sit there and look at it all day? "Eat your frog" is a popular expression that's been around for a long time. It has to do with procrastination, which results in poor planning and execution. The idea here is to make whatever you want to do the *least* the first thing you do each day. It gets it done plus clears your thought process from the distraction of needing (and dreading) to get it done.

NEGATIVITY

Making sure to avoid a culture of negativity is another key ingredient to increasing productivity and reducing inefficiency in your workplace. If constantly surrounded by negative input why would you have an expectation of creating positive results? Negativity spreads, employees' lack of effort is obvious, and company rules go by the wayside. If that's what you're picking up from your coworkers you need to figure out why and address it. While some people will respond to negative input, most people are going to eventually get worn down by it.

It's easy to make the assumption that your coworkers are the cause of the poor climate within a business but *you* could be what's making it hard to work at your business! Instead of constantly focusing on negative occurrences in the business, try to take those moments and turn them into something with a positive spin. The culture of your company has been well entrenched, so don't expect the changes you make, even if they're quick, simple, and positive, to immediately bring change. It will take time but by identifying and addressing the problems, you'll get there.

Don't Be Afraid to Ask for What You Want

Wayne Gretzky, one of the greatest hockey players of all time, once said, "You miss 100 percent of the shots that you don't take." So if you want something in life getting it might start with simply asking for it. This can apply to a promotion that you want and may be as simple as asking what it would take to get one. Overall it comes down to the fact that the worst thing you are likely to hear is "No." That being said, I know that the act of asking isn't as easy for some of us as it is for others. My suggestion when it comes to asking for a promotion, pay increase, or input about what you need to do regarding either is to do so in a structured way. Asking a manager or your boss for either in an unstructured way is certainly not going to end up the way you want.

So how do you go about this? It can be pretty easy. You should ask for a meeting with whoever's in charge of making this decision. I need to reemphasize the "decision maker" part. This person is likely to be busy much of or most of the time, so ask to do so at a time of their choosing. When that time arrives remember, it is up to YOU to be prepared. Have a list of questions handy or be ready to state your case in detail as to why you are ready or deserving of advancement.

Best Tips and Preparation Suggestions
- Prepare a list of reasons as to why you believe you deserve what you are asking for
- Treat yourself like a product or service that you are selling
- Present any and all information that sheds positive light on you, such as perfect attendance, high levels of production and so on
- Be prepared to NOT receive an answer on the spot
- Don't be argumentative, as this will sour your position
- Focus on solutions, not on problems
- If told no, then professionally ask what it will take to get what you want

- If told no while being given feedback take that as a favorable way of them telling you what you need to do

Do You Have a Career Plan?

So much of this book is about having a plan. Do you have one for yourself when it comes to your job? If you don't that might be one of the reasons you aren't getting what you want. Having a plan for your career is essential. You need to have an understanding of what you want and how you are planning on getting it. "I want to make more money!" is not a plan.

Here are some helpful questions to ask when planning your career path:

Where am I at right now?

What do I like doing?

What am I passionate about?

What do I really dislike doing?

What qualifications do I currently have?

What qualifications do I still need?

What are my professional strengths and weaknesses?

What are my characteristics that stand out the most?

What is my true definition of success?

What is my expected timeline for achieving benchmarks along the way?

Am I willing to do what it takes to get to this goal? Time, Money, Effort, Resolve.

LEADERSHIP, SPEAK UP

Earlier in the book I shared a story about my early days as a salesperson. As many of you are aware sales is a great way to make significant income. However, it wasn't until later in my career that I learned a path to even greater riches and fulfillment. What path is this I speak of? It is the path you create by being a leader at whatever it is that you do. So I have to ask . . . Are you a leader? It can be a tough question to answer. Think about it, are people ahead of you in the professional food chain exhibiting some kind of leadership attributes? The answer is most likely yes.

Leadership comes in many forms, and it is often difficult to appoint a leader. Simply holding a position that manages others doesn't actually make you a leader. It is important to acknowledge that. True leaders almost always have one or more of these traits:

POSITIVITY
CONFIDENCE
FOCUS
INTEGRITY
PASSION OR INSPIRATION
CREATIVITY OR INNOVATION
OPEN-MINDEDNESS
DECISIVENESS
DRIVE, RESOLVE, OR PERSISTENCE
RESPONSIBILITY OR ACCOUNTABILITY FOR THEIR
ACTIONS
STRONG ABILITY TO COMMUNICATE
ABILITY TO ACHIEVE GOALS THROUGH THE HELP OF
OTHERS

You don't have to possess *all* of the traits and attributes listed. In fact that would be pretty tough. But each of us has the ability to develop and build most of these traits in our own lives. Doing so is likely to help you in all facets of your life, not just professionally. So I challenge you from this moment forward to try and be a leader in whatever you do. It can and should have a remarkably profound impact on your life and those around you.

Focus on Solutions Instead of Problems

If I'm starting to sound like a broken record, it is because this point is really important! Pretty much anyone can identify a problem. What matters is the *solution!* Think about it for a minute. If you go into the manager's office where you work and say, "There is a problem with the production line!" you may have done a good job of alerting someone to the issue, but I ask you, where does the real value exist? It is in the solution to the problem! So now let's revisit that scenario. What if instead you walked into the manager's office and said, "There is a problem with the production line. We can fix it easily by changing the process that we are doing to X, Y, Z." Now *there* is someone who is producing value by presenting a solution. Overall your employer, employees, coworkers, and yourself all benefit most from the solution, not the problem. So try and catch yourself when thinking about or discussing a problem and not presenting a solution. In some ways you are just complaining or even being negative. The positive and productive person focuses on the solution!

LISTEN TO FEEDBACK

For many of us this is tough, but it's a crucial part of professional development. It is natural to in some way recoil from critical input. Yet this is where we are receiving the best input possible. Instead of responding poorly to feedback and input we should actually thank those who offer it. Whether it is about you as a professional, your workplace, or the service or product that you offer, this input can also inspire the solutions that you might need to offer your best.

ARE YOU TOO FOCUSED ON MONEY?

At first this might sound a little weird but it is something I want you to strongly consider. And doing so can really be a challenging thing. Many of us believe that our jobs are all about money and that *is* the end result of our actions and participation in our jobs. However, it is important to understand that money is a byproduct of the PROCESS. When we work we are engaging some kind of process, whether it be structured or unstructured. Looking at it this way we are then forced to consider how to improve the process or processes. Improvement means better results. Better results should lead to more money. So if your goal is to make more money as an employee or entrepreneur I must encourage you to focus on your processes.

Ask yourself:

What can I do to work more efficiently?
What can I do to increase my positive outcomes?
What can I do to help increase the productivity of those around me?
Are all of the things I do or processes even necessary?

By making simple adjustments you can make leaps forward at your job. Remember, your employer is most likely focused on your output. Start thinking about yourself as a production facility and now it is your job to improve the overall output. Yes this is a robotic way to view yourself at work but there is a reason that robotic processes exist in all major production facilities worldwide—they are efficient and fast!

IDENTIFY INEFFICIENCY

Nothing will increase your perceived value in the workplace more than being the person who regularly and consistently figures out ways to save the company money! Not only does that make you truly essential, it will also get the attention of those who decide whether or not you will receive promotions, pay increases, or bonuses. Remember, sometimes the most efficient decision is to eliminate a process altogether. Try and be mathematical and systematic when reviewing your own or your company's processes. Simple almost always wins as well.

SHARPEN YOUR TOOLS

Never stop learning! Part of me wants to just leave it at that, because that is truly the bottom line. It never ceases to amaze me when it comes to how many people seem to fear learning something new or feel like learning ended with their school graduation. Things change! We need to as well and that starts with learning. The amount of knowledge and information out there is more or less limitless. Access to this information is literally right in front of you online. During the process of building GigaBook I can't even begin to list how many new things I not only needed to learn but was forced to learn. No one was going to come along and hold my hand while I did either. The toughest part was that in many situations I didn't even know what I didn't know. So how did I do it? Research! Google is the ultimate professor in many of these classes too!

It is possible that learning through search engine research isn't what you need to achieve your career goals. So as a part of creating your career plan you might need to figure out what kind of continuing education or certification is useful to move your career forward or even maintain what you have now. The access to accredited online courses and classes is bigger and broader than ever before. In fact you even have access to programs from Ivy League schools through this very method, so don't limit yourself.

They Will Never Care As Much As You Do

It took me several years of frustration to finally except the fact the no one was ever going to care as much about my business as I did. I see this a lot with business owners and managers. We have an expectation that everybody who comes to work has the business's best interest at heart and will be passionate about what they do. I can't tell you how many afternoons and evenings I spent feeling frustrated, confused, and even angry at times because I just couldn't figure out why no one at my business seemed to care.

Do your employees and coworkers even have a reason to care? I know that seems like a really silly question, but outside of an hourly or salary paycheck do they really have a vested interest in the business's profitability and success? If they don't, you shouldn't be surprised when they don't seem to care. Of course I don't agree with people feeling this way. I've always been someone who prided myself on doing a good job, being reliable, and working toward the success of any business venture I've been involved. But the reality is no one's ever going to care as much as you do.

There is, however, a way to increase caring within your workplace. You either need to find a way to have your employees and coworkers share in the success of the business or at a minimum you have to begin to celebrate successes and victories *within* the business. This doesn't mean having a keg party on the loading dock every time the sales department makes a big sale. Praise, recognition, and incentives can go a long way toward the way your staff feels about your business. A person who feels appreciated will always do more than is expected.

STAY POSITIVE

Negative Nancy isn't a likely candidate for promotion. So getting where you want to be involves being positive! Positive people are more likely to gain attention for this trait, but also you will find others will have more interest in working with you. You are also more likely to achieve better results when you have a positive mindset about doing so!

HAVE POSITIVE AND PRODUCTIVE BODY LANGUAGE

How do you appear to everyone else at work? Remember, perception is reality on some level. So it is important for you to project winning and productive body language. Standing up straight and not slouching when seated are the foundation of positive body language. Here are a few things to consider:

Positive Body Language

- Having an upright posture
- Making eye contact
- Being genuinely engaged when others are speaking to you
- Giving a firm but not crushing handshake
- Positive motions like nodding your head
- Genuine reactions when appropriate, such as a smile
- Slow yourself down. If you seem like you are rushed it doesn't show interest

<u>Body Language to Avoid</u>
- Looking at your phone, laptop, or other device when in others' company
- Tapping, twitching, or fidgeting
- Fake smiles and reactions
- Being too close to those speaking to you
- Poor eye contact

PICK YOUR BATTLES WISELY

The worst battle to fight is the one that didn't need to be fought at all. Trying to carefully choose when to take a stand or be aggressive is really important when it comes to your career. While you want to be a leader and someone who produces solutions, make sure that you don't overdo it. This all comes back to developing the traits that effective leaders have and being positive. Always consider what you will gain if the result of the battle goes your way. Are you going to accidentally alienate everyone during the process of trying to make a point that wasn't even that important? Are you actually spreading negativity instead of producing a positive result? Is what you are trying to fix truly important or a high priority? Is what you are trying to fix even related to what you are supposed to be focused on?

Are you ready to take over the business world now? Hopefully so. You will find that following the advice from this section can really do a lot for your overall condition. While some say that "Money doesn't buy happiness," I would say that it does create "peace of mind" and isn't that just a different description of happiness? Improving your professional life will result in a better income, which reduces stress and anxiety about money. That extra cash then in turn allows you to be able to do the things that you might have listed in your goals, therefore creating a stronger sense of fulfillment and satisfaction. All of this relaxation and lack of anxiety leads to a healthier physical life. So let's move on to discussing that!

A Conversation with
CARSTAR Founder Lirel Holt

I had the pleasure of meeting Lirel Holt through my neighbor, coworker, and writing assistant Gail Jennings. She had worked with Lirel and the franchise he founded, CARSTAR, for nearly twenty years. The franchise was founded in 1989 and now represents the largest network of auto body shops in North America, with over 450 locations. How did it all start? In Lirel's own garage!

After our introduction, Lirel and I immediately seemed to be on the same page. Being two people who love talking about business and industry we breezed through a two-hour session at his office and had many subsequent e-mails and conversations as well. If you are someone who wants to start a business, then this is a conversation that you should pay attention to, as Lirel's story and success are about as great of an example as any of us can hope for.

MATT: What did you do to find balance in your life during CARSTAR's growth cycle? How did that impact your personal, professional, or physical life?

LIREL: There was little balance in building CARSTAR. It required focus and just about all the effort I could give. In order to have a family life with two little boys, I got up at 4:00 a.m. and went to the office. I could get more done between 4:30 a.m. and 8:00 a.m. than I could get the rest of the day. Being early gave me quiet time, no interruptions, and prepared me to be ahead of the questions and problems. At the end of the day, around 5:30 p.m., I'd leave the office and become a normal dad with the boys, going to their baseball games or school activities. By 9:00 I'd hit the sack with the aim to get going early again. I just didn't let myself get tired until I went to bed. Ben Franklin was right: "Early to bed, early to rise, makes a man healthy, wealthy, and wise."

As far as using my time, I had implemented my own "time management" procedures, which worked for me. One day our marketing manager and my VP came in and closed the door. I thought, *uh-oh*. They presented a better way for organization and time management that fit everyone. They firmly, but lovingly, forced me to get off my system and on the system they wanted as the company standard. I hated it at first, but loved it before long and it worked. We rolled it out to EVERY employee in the company and taught it as the very first course franchisees took when they came to Kansas City for training.

What are a few things about you and your background that my reader might find interesting?

Before CARSTAR, I had taught entrepreneurial business for several years. I taught cost accounting as well. The class became the highest rated course by the 3M Company.

While I was traveling and teaching business I decided to run a survey of business owners on the subject of stress. I wanted to know precisely what leaders believed caused stress in their life. I met a business owner in Boston, and hired him later at CARSTAR, who truly worked over one hundred hours a week. My premise was that the amount of hours worked would tie in directly with how much stress the person rated for themselves. The results of hundreds of surveys were surprising: *The amount of time they worked didn't tie directly to stress at all.*

I took the feedback and broke it down into many areas, one being how many hours they worked. Surprisingly, many that returned results stating they worked the most hours were the happiest and rated themselves as having low or moderate overall levels of stress. Finding this to be really interesting I dug deeper, as I was also curious about whether or not they had productive family lives too. The results surprised me yet again. Hours worked had less of a "direct" impact on how the person felt when it came to their family life.

After surveying and talking to over seven hundred leaders, owners, and managers from the US and

Canada, the survey showed that presidents and owners who had a lower level of stress had one thing and only one thing in common: profit. Those who were running companies that were making money rated themselves low stress. They loved the game. They were winning. Profitability gave the person the ability to leave work at any time and golf or see the family or spend time doing what they enjoyed. But the leaders were having so much fun winning they didn't want to be away from the business. They didn't view themselves as having stress and even found it odd that others would. They essentially thought they only had "problems" and most everything else was under control.

On the contrary, those leaders who rated themselves with ongoing, frustrating, and debilitating stress had the same thing in common, but in reverse. It wasn't the number of hours they worked. High levels of stress were tied directly to lack of profit. If they didn't make a profit their business as a whole was at great risk and they felt the pressure of that day in and day out. Many shared with me not being able to sleep, worrying about having to fire people they cared about, and the stress of not being able to make payments to the bank or vendors.

Conducting this survey changed my overall view when it came to balancing life. My original thoughts were wrong and reality was different than I anticipated. What

I found was the goal of business is profit and having profit makes business fun. Profit is what gives the leader freedom and flexibility, the choice of how you spend your time with whomever you choose.

Not having profit means you are losing. Therefore, the stress, anxiety, and everything else had a greater chance of wobbling out of balance at any time.

How did you handle moments of doubt, anxiety, or the intense stress that can be associated with a venture of that scale?

We took a long time, almost two years of planning, before we launched the business. We worked to get everything systematized and ready to operate. We applied "implication thinking." Basically we discussed a lot of scenarios for success and failure. "Okay, so if this *doesn't work*, what then? If it *works*, what then?"

Frankly at launch I was scared to death. My house and savings were all on the line. We knew the marketplace inside and out and I had credibility with many in the industry. Again, we had deeply planned and prepared to the extent our meager finances allowed. We went from zero to one hundred stores in less than eighteen months. I was traveling all the time as the main salesperson and the face of the company. At home we were training franchisees who were flying in to Kansas City and I was part of that when I wasn't selling on the road. Being a startup I had to be the guy who told and

172

sold people and then came home to help train them.

What input, comments, or other information do you have about the subject of success and life balance?

"You get what you focus on." That statement is almost always right. I focused on CARSTAR. The ability to focus means giving up other things. Understanding "delayed gratification" to get something built is one of the keys to long-term success at anything.

Focus seems to offset the concept of life balance. If everything is in balance, you don't move. Like being perfectly balanced standing in the middle of a teeter-totter, a movement to a focus on one side or the other will pull it out of balance.

I think some might say that work-life balance is about predictability. But being a really good president or CEO means taking advantages of opportunities. It means pushing for growth and putting yourself in situations and in areas that are highly unpredictable and risky hoping for the chance that you can make big leaps after.

When it comes to taking chances I have found this quote to be accurate: "Ships are safe in harbor, but that's not what ships are for."

SECTION SEVEN:

BALANCING YOUR MIND AND BODY

WITHOUT A HEALTHY mind and body nothing else really matters. Everything that we've discussed so far comes back around to the physical elements of our lives. When you have extraordinary stress in your personal or professional life it can have a severe impact on your physical being. Since I am not a doctor, dietician, or any other practitioner of medicine, I'm not going to give specific health or diet advice. What I *am* going to do is try and help you gain an understanding of the importance of physical health and how balance is interrupted without it.

I believe the following factors have the biggest influence on our physical being:

- Diet
- Activity
- Environmental factors
- Stress management
- Rest and relaxation
- Substance control
- Self-actualization
- Self-esteem

YOU ARE WHAT YOU EAT, RIGHT?

Then I am a chicken sandwich. In all seriousness, they had it right when they taught us this in elementary school. It's really basic. A healthy diet helps you have a healthy body. At the moment this is being written I am forty-one years old. I'm now one of *those* people who says, "Man it really was a lot easier twenty years ago." And it's true. So this part of our life is something we need to get better at as we age. I also admit, it's not my strong suit. Living in Kansas City, the home of the world's greatest barbeque, I have a weakness when it comes to ribs and other great food the local establishments serve. As a result, I provide myself with additional challenges when it comes to dieting. Did you see how that was phrased? *I provide myself with additional challenges when it comes to dieting.* I want you to consider that when you decide what to eat and when! If you choose to eat poorly then the result of that is a greater challenge when it comes to burning it off.

And in Second Grade You Said Math Would Never Be Useful

You don't need to be a scientist to understand how caloric input and output works. It is remarkably simple and easy to understand. Let me explain.

Take your body weight and multiply by ten. This is your estimated caloric output from just being alive and existing in a somewhat inactive state. Some institutions use eleven as the multiplier, but we are going to use ten because a) it's easier to remember and b) it gives us a slightly stricter standard.

Example: You weigh 150 pounds. So you will burn roughly 1500 calories (150 x 10) today regardless of if you exercise or not.

A pound of fat contains 3500 calories. So in order to lose one pound of fat you need to create a deficiency equal to 3500 calories over whatever span of time you use this formula. So taking the example above of 1500 calories, if you want to lose a pound of fat in a week, you will need to either consume 1000 calories a day for seven days, OR create additional output equal to 500 calories a day past the "break even" point of 1500 calories.

Therefore, what you put it your body compared to your output of energy without a doubt creates a very predictable result.

The last thing I am going to demonstrate takes a few high-calorie foods and then the amount and type of exercise it will take to expend that caloric input. Next time you have that handful of cookies you will be able to visualize what amount of activity and effort might be required to balance that out.

Right when you thought I would list candy, pie, and non-diet soft drinks I give you:

Raisins, a 1.5-ounce box –129 calories
Peanut butter, 1 tablespoon – 100 calories
Trail mix – up to 700 calories per cup

These are foods that most of us consider healthy!

Now let's get an idea about the average caloric output for a few common exercises. I do have to say these numbers can vary depending on the intensity at which they are performed and your total weight, so these are generalizations, not rigid numbers.

Projections are based on the same 150-pound individual we have been using.

Climbing stairs – approximately 9 calories a minute
Swimming – also approximately 9 calories a minute
Walking at a moderate pace – approximately 5 calories per minute

So that tiny box of raisins will require a twenty-six-minute walk to burn off, the teaspoon of peanut butter requires an eleven-minute swim, and the trail mix requires one hour and seventeen minutes of stair climbing! Were you expecting that? Now that we have a better understanding of the formula that affects our weight, let's talk about some ways you can increase your level of activity and caloric output.

Stay Active, Stay Healthy!

Without strengthening our body, we run the risk of weakening our minds. Therefore, the importance of staying active is crucial. I define "active" as putting your body in motion OFTEN. This can be done amid the many things you have going on in your life. Much like the other techniques presented in this book, small simple changes can in fact create big results in your physical life.

Here are a few tips for getting exercise and physical activity without making major changes:

TAKE THE STAIRS INSTEAD OF THE ELEVATOR
This is as straightforward as it sounds. Need I say more?

WALK AND TALK
Instead of sitting at your desk or on your couch when you make or take calls, put yourself in motion. You might need to buy a headset but outside of that it should be pretty easy to get this done. At a minimum stand up and pace in whatever space you are in.

PARK IN THE "WORST" SPOT
If you need more physical activity then the "worst" parking spot is actually the BEST spot! The upside of this change is that you won't need to compete for, or worry about finding a parking spot. Doing this results in you walking more. It's that simple.

STAND UP WHILE YOU WORK
This is really gaining a lot of popularity. Not only does the act of standing burn more calories than sitting, it has other health and productivity benefits too.

USE TECHNOLOGY
There are a whole lot of mobile apps and other wearable technology that can help you monitor your

levels of physical activity. TRY ONE! What these applications and devices do is encourage you to be a better version of your active self each day!

TAKE THE LONG WAY EVERY TIME

This one is pretty easy. In many ways it just means try not to be so lazy. While much of what we have discussed involves finding ways to be more efficient, this is the opposite. Find ways to stand up, walk, climb stairs, or whatever produces more activity in your regular routines. Go out of your way to travel the longer path when going about your daily life. If you are at your child's soccer game walk a lap or two around the field. I think you probably get the point.

According to the Centers for Disease Control and Prevention, there are *a lot* of benefits that come with increased activity.

- Easier to control your weight
- Reduction in the risk of cardiovascular diseases
- Reduction in the risk of type 2 diabetes
- Reduced risk of getting certain types of cancer
- Stronger bones and muscles
- Improvements in mental health and mood
- Increases your chance of living a longer life

How can you argue with that?

Here Comes Some Information You (Should) Already Know!

Now that you have a few tips about how to increase your level of activity without dedicating blocks of time to exercising, let me go ahead and say this. DEDICATE SOME TIME 4–5 DAYS A WEEK TO EXERCISE. I feel as if I need to at least mention that. I think each and every one of us understand its importance. It can be as simple as taking a walk around your neighborhood, or you might choose to do something else. Just do *something!*

Detoxify Your Surroundings

Everything around you has an impact on your well-being. This isn't limited to just the physical environment. It includes your mental environment and the situations and factors that influence your thoughts and actions.

You don't have to be a genius or doctor to see how specific factors in the physical environment can lead to your health or lack of. Air, water, and soil pollution, in addition to chemical exposure, climate change, or ultraviolet radiation can all be contributing factors to more than one hundred illnesses or diseases according to the World Health Organization.[6] We all know that on some level, so let's keep moving.

---

[6] By Focusing on Reducing Environmental and Social Risk Factors, Nearly a Quarter of the Global Burden of Disease Can Be Prevented.

What a lot of us might not consider is the impact that other types of "environments" have on our general sense of balance. These are often referred to as "toxic" situations, which feels really appropriate when referring to the term "environment." These are the situations, friendships, relationships, or other stuff around us that are polluted with negativity, failure, and a general lack of positive influence. Don't make the mistake of underestimating how powerful these "environmental" factors can be. The stress, distraction, and chaos these toxic factors provide in your life can quickly undermine your attempts to improve. I have more or less trained myself to seek and destroy the biggest and most regular sources of negativity around me. I recommend that you do the same. This sometimes requires tough decisions and resolute action, however it is necessary if you really do seek balance in your life.

REST AND RELAXATION

Yes, please! It is really important to unwind. This is easier said than done for some us, myself included. While it is important to put a valiant effort forward

---

Examples include Promoting Safe Household Water Storage, Better Hygiene Measures, Safer Management of Toxic Substances in the "Environmental Health." *World Health* Organization, n.d. Web 07 Nov. 2016.

when it comes to improvement, seeking balance, and overall achievement, sometimes you just need to chill out. This can and should occur in small, regular doses, but also needs to occur in larger intervals as well. Pause a few minutes and take it all in each day, and also make sure to regularly schedule breaks or vacations. I think that is all I really need to say here.

Today's Forecast, Cloudy with a Chance of More Clouds

This is what you can and should expect if you don't have a firm grip on substance. By "substance" I am referring to things that change or alter your state of mind when smoked or ingested. Whether it is alcohol, tobacco, weed, prescription medication, or something else, these substances can easily cast a cloud over you without your even knowing it. Are you one of those people who says, "I can still get up and work with a hangover!" Or maybe, "Pot doesn't affect my ability to do that!" Well I hate to be the bearer of bad news, but it does. Simply put, a clear mind is a healthy mind.

Now I'm not going to sit here and preach prohibition, but I am going say that the likelihood of you achieving your goals, gaining a sense of balance, and being happy in general is not going to improve by getting drunk or high regularly. Doing so casts a cloud over your ability to see things clearly, be energetic, or operate with a positive mindset. If you don't believe me try this challenge. Go "substance"-free for thirty days, no matter what it takes. If you can truly tell me that you DON'T feel better and have a clearer state of mind then I will admit defeat in your case, while acknowledging that you in fact can operate outside of the norm.

SELF-ACTUALIZATION

Doing what you feel you are capable of is about as powerful as it gets. In fact this feeling can even act as a short-term antidote during times of extreme imbalance. Self-actualization is commonly referenced when referring to the "Hierarchy of Needs" presented by Abraham Maslow, an American psychologist who was born in 1908 and died in 1970.[7]

This theory, which is often presented visually in the shape of a pyramid, is as follows:

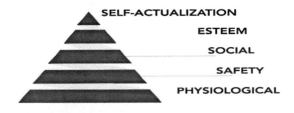

---

[7] https://www.psychologytoday.com/blog/hide-and-seek/201205/our-hierarchy-needs

Basic physiological needs. Those needs consist of basic requirements, such as air, food, and water. More or less the things that when not present or absent lead to our death.

Safety, such as personal, financial, or personal safety, including basic well-being or general protection from accidents or illness.

Social. This is where our needs become a bit more complex. Our sense of happiness or balance can be greatly affected or influenced by our need for acceptance within our peer groups, including friends, coworkers, and those we have general or intimate relationships with. Absence of this in our lives will eventually lead to increased anxiety, decreased feelings of happiness, and inability to move forward to the next level of Maslow's theory.

Esteem, or self-esteem, is present in all of us. It is the way we view ourselves, which then in turn has a strong influence on how we project ourselves to others. There are two levels of esteem, the lesser being the esteem that come from the feeling of being accepted and respected by others, then the more powerful version being the level at which we appreciate ourselves and respect ourselves within our personal, professional, and physical life. We will pick this up again shortly.

Then we have the pinnacle of Maslow's theory, *SELF-ACTUALIZATION.* This is feeling like you are either achieving or accomplishing all that you possibly can. That you are in fact being the BEST version of you possible. These achievements and accomplishments are absolutely different for each of us. They are often times deeply personal. Unfortunately, most people will not experience this feeling in their lifetime. You can. By clearly defining WHAT your definition of self-actualization is, then determining HOW you can get there, you too can embrace this feeling. I have experienced this feeling and it is truly pure. I don't want to spoil it for you, so that is all I will say. I felt self-actualized when I accomplished my lifelong goal of opening and running a highly-profitable business. Now once I did that and embraced the feeling of self-actualization I realized there was so much more that I wanted to do, and felt that I was capable. So I started writing it down, breaking it into achievable and doable tasks and got to work. That is part of the reason that I'm writing this book. Another reason being that I would love to see anyone use the process I did to get what they want out of life!

BEING A BETTER VERSION OF YOU

If every day a better version of you appeared, wouldn't that be great? It can happen. I find this concept to be powerful in all parts of life. And it's simple: *Every day try to do better than you did the day before.* You can make this an overall promise or divide it into personal, professional, and physical goals.

In practice, if one of your physical goals is to lose weight, then try eating better today than you did yesterday. Maybe you switch the usual side of fries to a salad. If one of your professional goals is to advance in the workplace then either do a better job at your position today than you did yesterday, or perhaps do something to improve the skills needed to advance. If your personal improvement goal is learning a foreign language, then spend a little more time studying today than yesterday.

As much as I love being positive with you, the reality is that you probably aren't going to win at this game *every* day. That is just fine—and part of being human. The goal here is to stay on track even after an inevitable setback or two. Achieving success in any part of your life involves the formation of quality habits. These small, but consistent improvements will accelerate your achievement process in remarkable increments. It will also prevent what I call the "negative slide:" the slow, or sometimes rapid, descent into the world of negative outcome.

This same concept can be used in a worldlier sense too. Try being a better overall human being than you were yesterday. I'm not saying that you are otherwise a bad person. However, being extra mindful of who we are can help us better become who we wish to be. Instead of ignoring trash on the ground, pick it up and drop it in a trashcan. Instead of getting angry at another driver on the way to work, just let it go.

To jumpstart your better self, here are some fun and interesting ways to enhance your life any day:

- Fix something that is broken at home
- List five things that you are grateful for

- Learn something new
- Stop complaining
- Set your alarm earlier
- Create a budget
- Start any kind of investment
- Limit yourself to thirty minutes of social media or video games
- Remove one unhealthy item from your diet
- Drink water instead of soda or coffee
- Get thirty minutes of exercise
- Write down something nice about your partner
- Say "I love you" to someone
- Give a hug to someone who needs one
- Make a new social connection
- Associate with someone you admire
- Try to catch yourself before being judgmental
- Do an anonymous good deed
- Be a better listener
- Don't compare yourself to others, just be you
- Go outside to enjoy fresh air
- Take twenty minutes and just sit in silence
- Say and do something optimistic
- Retry a vegetable you hated as a kid

- Admit to a mistake you made and commit to doing better next time
- Set a new goal in each category
- Think about why integrity matters
- Make a charitable donation
- Write a paragraph about how great your life really is
- Say five nice things to yourself about yourself
- Say five nice things to others
- Identify five things stopping you from getting where you want to be
- Go to bed an hour early
- Reflect on some of the best moments of your life
- Teach someone something useful
- Smile at everyone you see today
- Forgive yourself for something
- Forgive someone else for something
- Avoid any and all gossip
- Take responsibility for something you failed at
- Be remarkably humble
- Watch a motivating speech from a movie or real life
- Call an old friend
- Only offer solutions, not problems

- Clean up something at your home that really needs it
- Write down your dreams, hopes, and ambitions
- Delete all of your unread e-mails
- Wash, dry, and fold ALL of your dirty laundry
- Google "How to improve self-image"
- Google "Ways to save money"
- Complete five to-do list items
- Define three things you have been procrastinating and do them without hesitation
- Do something "green" for the environment
- Learn how to fix something
- Take a different route to and from work
- Throw away or donate something you have been storing that you will never use again
- Do something that is outside your comfort zone
- Listen to a song that you find to be motivating
- Don't create any plastic waste
- Don't watch any television
- Sing loudly in the car on the way to work
- Do something completely selfless
- Consider what it is like to be everyone else you meet today

- Seek the wisdom of someone else and be genuine when learning/listening
- Take ten deep breaths each hour
- Go out of your way to say thanks to someone
- Address a problem that you have been neglecting
- Do something spontaneous
- Appreciate and reach out to an elderly person
- Be a friend to someone you believe may be lonely
- Make ten positive affirmations
- Turn off your phone for at least an hour
- Don't listen to, read, or watch the news today
- Eat meat-free for a day
- List five people, then write down something good about each one
- Don't consume any caffeine
- Look at old photos
- List five personality qualities you admire, then emulate them
- List five businesses that you would like to own
- Forbid negativity
- List five of your strengths
- Catch yourself arguing and STOP

- Tell yourself why you are awesome
- Make zero excuses today
- Make plans to attend a concert
- Pick a non-alcoholic drink option tonight
- Don't eat processed foods today
- Plant a tree or something that will grow for a long time
- Get a massage
- Buy a daily multivitamin
- Catch yourself being impatient on some level and stop
- Google three Yoda quotes
- Ask someone for personal feedback
- Review your retirement plan
- Draft an exercise plan
- Find some new music and jam out
- Visualize yourself being successful at three things
- Dress nicer than you normally do
- Buy a book of inspirational quotes
- Stand up straight and tall all day
- Work for one hour standing up
- Clean out your car
- Clean out your garage
- Go to an art museum
- Stop yourself every time you want to say, "I can't"

- Do something that scares you
- Make a list of five places you want to visit
- Make a list of five things you want to do
- Acknowledge that you can always improve
- Learn something new about money and finance
- Identify three ways that you can reduce spending
- Start a change jar and add to it daily
- Create a financial goal for the short term
- Create a financial goal for the long term
- Review all of your bills and see if they are for needs or wants
- Create a priority list for debt repayment
- Find an energy inefficiency in your home and fix it
- Replace a regular light bulb with an LED
- Learn three things about negotiating
- Recycle something
- See what you can do to improve your credit score
- Don't say any swear words today
- Hold hands with your partner for a while
- Ask your partner how their day was and then listen
- Ask your partner if there is anything you can help them with

- Put your phone in the other room, or leave it in your car for four hours
- Delegate three tasks to someone else
- Create a to-do list
- Look at three things you do often and make them more efficient
- Do your three most important tasks today
- Do the thing you have been procrastinating the most FIRST
- Clean up something cluttered around you
- Take a walk
- Schedule an activity with your kids
- Evaluate your personal relationships
- Read about different personality types
- When you want a snack, ask yourself if you are just bored
- Make eye contact with everyone today

You Have What It Takes to Be Amazing! Seriously!

The final component of a balanced physical being is self-esteem. This is your assessment of your worth, talents, appearance, intelligence, and overall ability to DO things! Absence of positive self-esteem will make it remarkably difficult for you to find balance in your life. A healthy view of ourselves is paramount in our ability to believe that we can in fact have everything we feel we need to be happy.

Poor or low levels of self-esteem are the gateway to a number of common and unfortunate situations in many people's lives. It can lead to or is present in people experiencing clinical depression. It is likely to result in prolonged states of underachievement, causing us to fall well short of our goals. In severe instances it may lead to tolerance of abusive relationships and situations.

Too much self-esteem, on the other hand, can create a sense of entitlement that seems all-too-common in today's society. It also shields our critical ability to learn and grow from our mistakes. People with too high of an opinion of themselves often times have a hard time getting along with others.

So where do we find balance with all of this? Well hopefully at this point in the book you realize that you do in fact have everything you need to achieve happiness. Since self-esteem is a needed component of that happiness, it too should have balance. This requires us to humble ourselves. That is where the balance in your self-esteem stems. It involves us on many levels surrendering to the fact that we all have flaws. That means you, me, and everyone else in the world. Without this recognition you cannot achieve balanced self-esteem and therefore a balanced life.

So what is the secret here? It starts with the conversation we have with ourselves all day, every day. We visited this subject in the first section of this book, however it is so vital that I feel like I need to mention it again. If all we do is tell ourselves that we suck, then guess what, we will. Catch yourself in these moments and replace those negative comments with ones that instead have a positive message. The more you improve the dialogue inside your mind, the faster your life will improve.

Next, stop comparing yourself to everyone else. It's not practical or reasonable to do so. We each operate in our own reality. Since there is only one of you, it is therefore impossible to fairly and accurately make these comparisons. Instead focus on your strengths and continue to be that better version of yourself each day.

Another fast way to higher levels of self-esteem is through working on improving each of the categories we explored. Get more exercise, eat better, try harder at work, or strive for improvements in your personal life. All of these lead to improved confidence and therefore an improved view of ourselves.

Giving is living! Helping other people get what they want out of life can help you do the same. I believe this to be a really powerful principle not only when it comes to building higher levels of self-worth but also when it comes to overall achievement. It speeds the process and quality of your own achievements while at the same time produces a remarkably satisfying feeling of knowing that you helped others. If you want to really take it to the highest level, start giving or doing without any expectation of return. This is hard to do, but when done it is truly the purest form of giving.

Lastly, focus on the things in life you *can* control. This means removing any expectation of perfect performance and accepting that no matter how good you are at something you will experience failure on some level. You can't control everything around you, and you can't undo things that you have already done. Within your control are thoughts, actions, decisions, attitude, effort, and many of the other subjects that I addressed in this book. Spending any effort or energy worrying about or fretting over things out of your ultimate control does nothing other than distract you from being able to achieve or realize your full potential.

Look, I most likely haven't met you. However, I am certain that you can in fact achieve happiness and an improved feeling of balance. We all can. Trying to make improvements in your life can and should be fun. Yes, it's going to be hard. Yes, it is going to take work, dedication, and mindfulness. But if you are willing to do what it takes, it certainly is out there for you. Hopefully you enjoyed our time together and found several things that stick with you and produce lasting and positive change. I really do want that for you and, more importantly, you should want that for yourself too!

AUTHOR'S NOTE

Over the last fifteen years, I've gone through an interesting journey. I've lived in Colorado, New Mexico, North Carolina, Washington, DC, and Indiana, and then came back to where it all began for me, Kansas City. During the early adult part of that timeline I worked at several different jobs in the music industry, not as a musician, but instead in the world of musical instruments. During that time, I was a senior manager of a chain of musical instrument stores, I helped open a chain of piano stores, and then went on to work as a district manager for Roland, the world's largest manufacturer of electronic music instruments.

Despite finding a lot of success at an early age, I couldn't handle it anymore. I wasn't balanced. All the travel and work started to take its toll on me. I went through a divorce, which resulted in going from feeling like I was years ahead of my peers to instead feeling like I was years behind. So in 2008 I decided to reinvent myself. Several people told me that I was crazy. I was about to quit a job that most people work their whole life to get, not knowing what I was going to do next. Having already quit jobs that people work their entire career to get I was told that I was forming a "bad pattern." But I knew I needed a change.

So at the young age of thirty-three I quit my job at Roland and went back to school. Why not, right? After a year in school and a growing need to NOT go broke from school expenses and a lack of income, I started exploring a whole lot of ways that I could possibly make money working online. After trying out several things I came across the secondary event ticket industry. Having just come out of the music industry this felt like a natural fit. So I started buying and selling concert tickets. Once again with a contingent of friends and family telling me that I was nuts, I felt differently about it. At the time I was far from financially stable; in fact I had a negative net worth. But what I did have was an American Express card with an eight thousand-dollar limit. Yep that's it. So off I went to try and take over the event ticketing industry.

You will have to buy me a beer to get all the details out of me, however what I will tell you is that it went well. I went from buying a few Taylor Swift tickets here and there and selling them on StubHub, to instead working myself into deals with sports teams and venues, helping sell their excess or premium merchandise on the secondary market. At one point, in the extra bedrooms of my modest home I was running a business that was grossing millions of dollars in revenue. It was pretty crazy. I still own that business today. It's grown up a lot and also moved out of my home. It has certainly been a fulfilling education, more so than the classes I quit in order to focus on it full-time (once again being told I was crazy). But I have to say that I wouldn't trade anything in exchange for all the lessons about business building, entrepreneurship, and hard work I gained along the way.

During the process of building my ticket business I continued trying new and innovative ways to make money. As a result, I opened an office in Cebu City, Philippines, where I still have several employees, most of whom have five or more years of service time with my company. This led to many successes and "attempted successes (failures)" with web development. The most notable creation being GigaBook.com, which is my professional pride and joy. Founded in 2013 out of a desire to make online booking services accessible and affordable for ANY small business owner, GigaBook turns your website into a booking engine for a minimal cost. The result is that our users are able to create more balance in their life by not feeling so chained to their business. By no longer having to deal with the burden of clients texting, calling, or leaving message at all hours, I realized that our users were really increasing their level of happiness, while increasing their profitability. And it only took eighteen thousand hours of development. I'm being sarcastic there, since you can't truly hear my tone.

So how and why is all of this relevant to "life balance." Well, I've had to learn to create a lot of it over the last fifteen years of my life. From my time traveling all over the Midwest, to reinventing myself at thirty-three, to creating multiple successful businesses, I learned a lot. I guess I should also mention that I'm a father and husband as well. Basically, I consider myself to be a super achiever. I get the work done of four people. I have people asking me how I do it. So I started really documenting it. The result is *Balance Me*.

I truly do believe that all who read the book will benefit from the same concepts and thought processes that help me find so much success.

ACKNOWLEDGMENTS

I wouldn't be following my own advice if I didn't take some time to acknowledge and thank those who helped make *Balance Me* happen.

First off, every bit of love, praise, and appreciation in me goes out to my beautiful wife, Jill. Your patience and understanding not only during the creation of the book, but also with me over the years, can't be described with just words. THANK YOU for always letting and encouraging me to be me!

Also need to thank my writing assistant and coworker Gail Jennings. Your calm and organized demeanor was the perfect balance for my oftentimes unbridled enthusiasm for this project. I am sorry, and you are welcome for all of the information, opinions, ideas, rants, craziness, and times when I needed to just talk out loud until I figured it out. You really did provide the structure this project needed.

For the creation of our amazing cover art, Krista Vossen you are a kind and patient woman. Your creativity and obsession with making everything perfect ended with exactly that result.

Lastly, thank you Patrick Price, who in my opinion is the greatest book editor alive. Yes, I only know one book editor, however I'm still fairly certain that you are better than all of the others. You taught me how to use my voice. So many people won't believe that because they already think I talk too much, but that isn't the voice I'm speaking of. Your ability to give me the courage, tools, and encouragement I needed to make this "MINE" was unbelievable. Thank you!

ABOUT THE AUTHOR

Matt DeCoursey is the founder and CEO of GigaBook, and also owns and operates other businesses. *Balance Me* is his first book, but won't be his last. He lives in Kansas City with his wife, son, and daughter. Visit Matt at www.mattdec.com.

CPSIA information can be obtained
at www.ICGtesting.com
Printed in the USA
FFOW05n0521100217